Praise for *Wake-Up Calls*

"Women tend to face unique challenges in funeral service. The book helps managers, leaders, and female staff members plot the path toward long and satisfying careers."

—John J. Horan, CFSP, chairman, Funeral Excellence Group; senior vice president, Park Lawn Corporation

"I wish I had this information available to me fifteen years ago. I felt the content was suspenseful, heartfelt, and all too familiar. Lisa's knowledge and support has been monumental in helping me overcome these industry challenges."

—Julie Bishop, co-owner and funeral director, Crevasse's Simple Cremation

"A smart, honest, and vulnerable story of unmatched resilience. Prepare to be inspired to unleash your greatness!"

—Allyse R. Worland, CFSP, owner, Have License Will Travel

"Lisa's book provides an authentic sharing of vulnerability, lessons learned, and inspiration. She offers insight into the challenges she encountered, and the manner in which she gracefully overcame them. This book was written from an honest place with an open heart."

—Dr. Jennifer Lares, CFSP, founder, Mulling Mortician, LLC

"*Wake-Up Calls* is a vital read for today's deathcare professionals. Lisa Baue draws on decades of leadership to offer a candid, forward-thinking look at the challenges we face, from staffing shortages to shifting consumer expectations. Her insights are especially timely as more women enter and shape the future of our profession. This book is an essential guide for those committed to leading with authenticity, adaptability, and purpose."

—Barbara Kemmis, executive director, Cremation Association of North America

"*Wake-Up Calls* is a fabulous guide for any professional looking to improve their leadership ability. Learning from failure is key, and Lisa describes many obstacles she had to overcome when she was suddenly thrown into running her family's funeral home with the untimely and completely unexpected death of her father, her role model who she cherished dearly. Lisa shares hard decisions she has made and encourages readers to take steps to avoid the problems her family business encountered."

—**Kathy Kelley,** CFO, family member owner,
and treasurer, Answering Service for Directors (ASD)

"Lisa's raw honesty and passion to mentor others is an inspiration. Her story, with its challenges, quest for learning, and drive to succeed in a profession dominated by men, will help others see what is possible when you answer those wake-up calls."

—**Cindy Foree,** executive director, Southern Cemetery,
Cremation & Funeral Association and Cemetery
Association of Tennessee; retired COO, Family Legacy

"*Wake-Up Calls* is the book I wish I had when I stepped into leadership after the loss of my parents and took on the responsibility of running our family's funeral business. With honesty and heart, it speaks to the challenges and triumphs women face, reminding us that we need more than resilience. We need mentorship, community, and a voice at the leadership table. It also candidly addresses the work–life balance so many of us navigate while running businesses, raising families, and caring for others."

—**Alicia Carr,** president and CEO, Kelco Supply Company

"In *Wake-Up Calls*, Lisa delivers a masterclass on resilience, leadership, and the unexpected journey of leading a family business with little preparation but much determination to succeed. Through candid storytelling, she shares the highs and lows of building a top-tier independent funeral organization and the impactful lessons learned along the way. Her passion for mentoring and empowering women in funeral service shines throughout, making this a must-read for any woman ready to lead, grow, and rise."

—**Rob Paterkiewicz**, executive director and CEO,
Selected Independent Funeral Homes

"In this heart-based resource, Lisa Baue reflects on a momentous career in funeral service. Her keen observations and insights paint a picture of both where funeral service has been and where it should also look to practice strategic change in the future. This book will inspire all of those who love and believe in funeral service to be the best they can be when serving families. Read this book and allow Lisa's 'wake-up calls' to lead the way."

—**Alan D. Wolfelt**, PhD, author; founder and director,
Center for Loss and Life Transition

"Lisa Baue has long been a pioneer for women in funeral service, and in *Wake-Up Calls*, she becomes a mentor to all of us. Through powerful storytelling and honest reflection, she offers a deeply personal blueprint for leadership rooted in grit, empathy, and purpose. I saw so much of my own experience in these pages, and I believe others will too. This book is a gift to the next generation of leaders and a wake-up call to the profession we all love."

—**Leili McMurrough**, president and program director,
Worsham College of Mortuary Science;
licensed funeral director and embalmer; licensed attorney

"A poignant and inspirational story of toughness, resiliency, and grit that is an inspired look at funeral service, leadership, and the importance of relying on friends, family, and colleagues in facing numerous challenges and being a trailblazer. A reminder that leadership in deathcare and in any profession is as much about empathy as it is about excellence."

—**Jedd Lapid**, executive director, Funeral Service Foundation

"Reading *Wake-Up Calls* felt like sitting with Lisa in a quiet room, sharing a glass of wine, and hearing her story unfold with warmth, honesty, and heart. Lisa's words are so personal, raw, and real. It was as if she were speaking directly to me, not just as a colleague, but as a fellow woman navigating the unique challenges and rewards of funeral service.

Lisa's journey reminded me how powerful mentorship can be, and how important it is for us as women in this profession to lift each other up. I found myself not only learning more about her but also learning more about myself—as a professional, a leader, and a woman. She shares her vulnerability, insight, voice, and above all, her leadership. This book is a gift to all of us walking this path, those who are in the height of their careers and those just beginning."

—**Danielle Knapp**, CEO, Iowa Funeral Directors Association

"As a leadership facilitator for over 30 years, one of the most important pieces of leadership—from my perspective—is authenticity. Lisa writes this book with incredible authenticity and transparency, sharing her life story with the untimely death of her father, buying the family business, and sharing the truth about her mistakes and shortcomings as a business owner. She learned through the "school of hard knocks" and never gave up, gritting through it all with incredible heart and absolute dedication to the funeral profession. She truly is the "poster child" for heart and grit! She shares her story with such transparency, especially for women to find inspiration and motivation to live their passion. More importantly, Lisa continues to dedicate her time and heart to the continued success of women in the funeral profession. Excellent read!"

—**Marguerite Ham**, founder and owner, Igniting Success

"Lisa Baue has been a trailblazer and passionate advocate for women in the funeral profession, paving the way for countless women to find their place and thrive in this field. For years, she has dedicated herself to creating an environment where women are empowered to lead, serve families with empathy, and pursue meaningful, lifelong careers.

Anyone who has worked with Lisa cannot help but notice her deep passion for the profession. As someone who has worked under her leadership, I can sincerely say she invests heavily in lifelong learning and personal growth, not just for herself but for her entire management team. She is committed to hiring the best, training the best, and being the best.

Lisa is a true visionary. She has constantly sought innovative ways to serve families better—through impeccable facilities, staff professionalism, and a relentless focus on excellence. One of her most powerful commitments has been to train her team to be 'courageous recommenders,' individuals confident enough to offer personalized and meaningful experiences to grieving families.

She believes that women bring unique gifts to the profession: compassion, empathy, and the willingness to go the extra mile. Lisa wants women to know they can build lifelong, rewarding careers in funeral service. For Lisa, being ordinary is never an option. She believes in setting a high bar, leading with tough love and modeling servant-hearted leadership.

Lisa has a generous heart. She believes that the 'little things' are actually the big things—and she inspires her staff to embrace the same philosophy, encouraging them to go above and beyond for the families they served.

When Lisa said she was publishing *Wake-Up Calls* to share her story, I was eager to read every word. While she is known for being tough, what many don't see is how deeply she cares. Her commitment to families and her staff is unmatched. She believes the best leaders are those who lead with a 'Servant's Heart.' It has been a privilege to work with Lisa. She is a fierce advocate for women, constantly encouraging them to stretch, lead, and mentor others. She lifts women up and challenges them to strive to achieve great things—and for that, so many of us are deeply grateful."

—**Pam Gehrs,** former director of sales and marketing,
Baue Funeral Homes, Crematory, and Cemetery;
area vice president of sales, Park Lawn Corporation

"*Wake-Up Calls* is an essential read for anyone in the funeral and deathcare profession—especially those in or aspiring to be in leadership roles. It's a call for empathy, equity, and evolution in a field that often demands so much, both personally and professionally. Lisa's storytelling and visionary leadership combine to create a work that is both moving and motivating. For anyone seeking to lead with integrity, care for their colleagues, and shape a more supportive future in the funeral profession, this book is both a guide and a gift."

—**John Heald,** chief growth officer, Legacy.com

A JOURNEY OF LEARNING
TO LEAD AND SUCCEED IN THE
FUNERAL AND DEATHCARE PROFESSION

Wake-Up
Calls

LISA BAUE

RIVER GROVE
BOOKS

Published by River Grove Books
Austin, TX
www.rivergrovebooks.com

Distributed by River Grove Books

Design and composition by Greenleaf Book Group
Cover design by Greenleaf Book Group
Cover images used under license from ©Adobestock.com

Publisher's Cataloging-in-Publication data is available.

Print ISBN: 978-1-966629-43-6

eBook ISBN: 978-1-966629-44-3

First Edition

I dedicate this book to all the women in my profession who have paved the way for our right to be seen, heard, and acknowledged as leaders. This book is also dedicated to their families, the owners and managers in the profession who supported them, and those who continue to do so today.

Contents

Introduction

I have spent my life working in the funeral profession, and I believe wholeheartedly in its value. I also know firsthand its many challenges. Through my work and life, I've been given a deep sense of purpose. I've also received a number of wake-up calls, each of which helped me grow as I learned to better use my head, my heart, and my grit to navigate the challenges and changes facing me. These wake-up calls taught me how to be a better person and a better leader. And now I would like to offer that learning to others in my profession to help them grow and thrive.

The truth is that funeral service can be incredibly difficult, in part because of the nature of our work but also because of current leadership practices and the often-negative work cultures they create. The profession at large needs a wake-up call—a massive one—because it's failing to serve the needs of its workforce, especially the large numbers of women within it. By doing so, it's also failing itself as a profession. When we cannot care for our own people in the ways they need most, we will not be able to do our best to care for the grieving families we serve.

I want to do what I can to help nudge the current leadership forward into the future. I want to advocate for positive change and encourage others working in the profession to speak up and advocate for themselves if they do not feel supported. Most of all, though, I want to support the next era of professionals in navigating their challenges and becoming strong leaders who advance and nourish their own careers, lives, and teams. Ultimately, I believe this approach is what will revitalize the profession itself.

It is important to support and encourage both men *and* women in this growth, as all groups are needed and essential to the profession. Recently, though, I have felt a deep calling to focus my energies primarily on supporting women in their growth as leaders in deathcare. A big part of that calling is because it is women who compose the largest group now coming into funeral service. It is women who have been telling me for the last five years they need more support, resources, and someone to talk to—women who have been telling me they need help developing themselves as leaders, finding their voices, and living in what is still mostly a man's world of funeral service.

In 2024, 75 percent of mortuary science graduates were reported to be women according to the American Board of Funeral Service Education (https://abfse.org). Women—along with a growing number of individuals from diverse minority groups and the LGBTQ+ community—are predicted to make up the future of our profession, yet the conditions prevalent in funeral service are often incompatible with what they need and desire in a workplace to become successful. This diverse group of the next era in the profession do not think the same, nor are their needs the same as those of the current Baby Boomer and Gen X owners and managers. These younger professionals want a better work–life balance and do not want to be on call every other night and continuously working nights and weekends. They also desire a fairer wage that is, at the very least, comparable to salaries in other professions. They—along with everyone in deathcare—deserve these kind of work conditions, yet they don't often seem to find them. No current statistics are available as of the writing of this book, but based on what I hear and what other leaders predict, we believe close to 50 percent of women are leaving our profession within five years of employment.

Many individuals are coming into funeral service to make a difference in the lives of those who are mourning their loved ones' deaths. They are often drawn by their own past experiences of grief and loss, along with a desire to work in a caregiving profession. Yet instead of welcoming them with arms wide open, our profession seems to be making it more difficult for them to remain and grow as future leaders.

How do I know about the obstacles women and others face in our profession today? I know because I spent more than forty-four years as a funeral director and thirty-eight of them as the CEO and owner at my family business, Baue Funeral Homes, Crematory, and Cemetery, in St. Charles, Missouri. I know because since selling my business in 2019, I have become a coach and mentor to this next era of funeral service leaders. At national conventions, in women's programs, and in our one-on-one calls, they are seeking solutions and advice. I listen. I have heard their concerns, their pain, and their stories of the horrible cultures they are working in and considering leaving; some of them are so frustrated that they are moving to other professions. I have heard their stories about uncaring owners and managers and the often-disgusting behavior they have to put up with in the workplace. It breaks my heart.

Before I went through my own wake-up calls as a funeral director and owner, I was part of the general leadership problem. A number of years into my journey as a funeral-home owner, I received a

360-degree evaluation from my staff and learned I had been letting them down. They did not feel I truly cared for them. I was so busy trying to run a rapidly growing business in a community whose population and death rate were exploding, I was not paying attention to what my team members' true needs were. So I made the determination to learn to become a different leader, a better leader, one who listened and cared deeply for each staff member at Baue's.

I hired a personal leadership coach, and I added consistent leadership training for all team members, including myself, as part of the regular curriculum in our company. We learned together how to become better leaders of ourselves and others. When I did this, I began to see our culture change. Our retention rate grew to more than 98 percent toward the last ten years of my ownership, our client family satisfaction grew to new levels we had never experienced before, and our business experienced exponential growth! When I learned to become a mentor and coach for members of team Baue, one who cared more for my staff than I did for business profits and even our client families, my company became the most successful it had ever been in its history. We became a company that nourished leadership at all levels while the number of women entering our company began to grow at greater and greater rates. The addition of leadership development for diverse people of all genders and ethnicities at Baue's changed our business for the better, helped us become the employer of choice, grew our market share and our profitability, and, most of all, improved the work and personal lives of members of team Baue!

While some other owners and managers in the profession have also found a path into heart-centered compassionate leadership, I have found that most continue doing things the way they have always been done, which is no longer working. It's no longer good enough. It is my hope that the current generation still in ownership and leadership will soon wake up or transition their businesses to new leaders who understand the evolving needs of the next era of staff entering our profession. But whether or not they step forward into their own responsibility to change, I will continue to do all I can to help develop and promote leadership programs for women, minority groups, and everyone seeking to grow in the profession of deathcare and funeral service in order for both them and the profession to thrive and succeed.

HEAD, HEART, AND GRIT

Everyone currently feeling unsupported in the profession needs to become their own advocate. And I especially want to see my own gender—which so often experiences more pressure to go along with the status quo—do more to speak up and ask the current leaders to listen and to challenge them to change. As individuals, we need to do better developing ourselves as leaders and designing our own path forward. And then, once we step into roles as managers and owners, we also need to lead ourselves and support our team members with integrity and maturity, using a combination of head, heart, and grit.

During my career, I had to learn to use all three of these attributes to become the best leader I could be, and when I made mistakes, I learned from those, too. I struggled with my own self-confidence many times, but my learned grit—aka courage—and heart for serving others kept me pushing through. And I eventually learned that without also leading with my heart first and foremost, none of the rest would matter. I could never truly be successful unless my leadership style evolved to care for my team members as much as, if not more than, the families we served. As an owner, I became passionate about caring for and supporting the women and the men of team

Baue, many of whom tell me, even today, that feeling valued and listened to back then helped them become the leaders they are today.

At Baue's, our leadership team grew to more than 65 percent female. This pattern has continued to grow, and I have been told they are now closer to 75 percent women. All four of their locations are managed by women, along with their care and cremation center and their preplanning sales team. These women who I spent time caring for, coaching, and developing became one of the core reasons our company was so successful. Many of them are still with the company today, and some have moved on to other firms or roles where they now hold leadership positions in regional and national companies. They tell me their leadership development experience, along with the mentoring and coaching they received at Baue's, contributed to their current success. I am so very proud of all of them. Not to leave our guys out—they, too, were and still are great leaders in their areas of expertise and leadership. Together, they became incredible team players, highly emotionally intelligent businesspeople who cared more for each other than they did for their individual success. And I was, and still am, so very proud of them.

After selling Baue, I remained passionate about helping develop the future leaders in our profession. And as I stepped into coaching and worked with more and more women, I realized this was where I felt most committed to making an impact. Today, I am dedicated to mentoring and offering support to the next era of women in the profession. I want to help everyone who is struggling in funeral service to learn to thrive, advocate for better working conditions, and develop themselves to become the leaders they want to be. Too often, I see women in our profession remain silent because they don't want to be seen as difficult. But it's time to speak up. I want to see them tap into their self-confidence, learn how to be more resilient, advocate for themselves, and help their employers understand their needs—all in a professional and empathetic manner. I want to see women be given a chance to develop the skills to become the strong, savvy, and heart-centered leaders I know our profession truly needs. I want to see them not just survive but *thrive*—and, in doing so, contribute in meaningful ways to the future success of the profession.

FUNERAL WOMEN LEAD

I hope this organization I helped start (https://funeralwomenlead. org) becomes part of the legacy I leave to the profession: helping those in the minority—mostly women—learn to lead, succeed, and thrive in our profession, which, though challenging them to greatness, offers so much to the world of deathcare. Yet I cannot do it alone. I am just one person, one small business coach. It will take a movement on a larger scale. And so in the latter half of 2024, I joined forces with a few other like-minded women—and a couple of great men, too—to start a foundation dedicated to developing the women leaders of the future.

We named it the Funeral Women Lead Foundation, and through it, we will be working to provide affordable and scholarship-based ongoing training and support with a women-focused leadership academy, an annual wellness summit, a coaching and mentoring program, a resource hub, a career center, and an online community that is a private and safe place for support and sharing to assist women in all stages of their professional development. We will continue listening to women and diverse minorities to discover their needs through valid research. We will also work to support other groups and associations that provide programs to help women, and we will work to provide continuing resources to our members that create more awareness of the opportunities for them to gain knowledge and grow into the leaders of tomorrow. If you would like to be more involved in this women's leadership support movement, you can connect with the Funeral Women Lead Foundation by scanning the QR code at the back of this book.

Together, we can make a difference in our profession to become better—not to just survive, but to thrive.

As part of my ongoing mission to support women in the profession, I've also written this book to share what I have learned over a lifetime in funeral service. In these pages, I hope you will find encouragement and inspiration that help you grow and thrive. I hope as I share my own story of growing (and many times failing) as a leader—learning to always draw upon my head, my heart, and my grit—you will learn, too.

I enjoyed a long, successful, and rewarding career in funeral service. I never could have done it without a powerful group of coaches, mentors, and supporters, many of them who are still on team Baue and some who continue to be active in the profession today. My wish for this book is that it offers you a piece of the learning and mentorship I was blessed to receive from both male and female mentors. I encourage you to seek out further support, whether through the Funeral Women Lead Foundation or other supportive programs that provide education, mentoring, and coaching.

I will not pretend that this profession is an easy path to success, but if you love the funeral, cremation, and burial business and believe, like I do, that it is worthwhile, compassionate, necessary work to support those who mourn, then I hope you will try to navigate its challenges and realize your goals and dreams. I hope you will become an advocate for better leadership training and development for both yourself and those you work with both now and in your future as part of the next generation. I hope you will reach out to find support and mentorship, work to develop your own self-confidence, learn to find your grit, and develop skills using both your head and your heart. I also hope you will learn to find your voice and advocate to have the important and needed conversations that help the current generation of owners and managers change our work through culture improvement. And I hope you persevere to becoming a powerful, empathetic leader, regardless of your gender, your ethnicity, or your chosen path in the profession, in a way that helps deathcare thrive and move forward successfully.

Lastly, I hope you embrace this book with an open mind. Not all of the lessons I learned along the way were fun ones. I am human, and I made many mistakes. It took a lot of grit, understanding, support, and forgiveness of myself and from and for others, in addition to finding self-awareness and the self-compassion I needed to survive and thrive through it all. Being an owner in general was and is not easy. Being a woman owner in a male-dominated profession was and still remains especially difficult. In my career, I made many sacrifices. I missed countless moments with my children and family. I did not have much time to dedicate to my own needs. At many junctures in my life, I sacrificed too much for the sake of business success and had very little time to seek a better work–life balance. Yet through these mistakes, I learned critical lessons along the way that made me a better person, mom, boss, business leader, and wife to my incredibly caring and supportive husband, Monte.

Now, I am sharing with you what I learned mostly the hard way, the lessons and wake-up calls I experienced, survived, and learned from. It is my hope they will be of benefit to you and generations to come. In this spirit, I've also included reflection questions at the end of each chapter to help you open into the lessons and gifts of your own life.

I wish each of you the gifts of open-mindedness, learning, leadership growth, heartfelt service, the desire to pay it all forward, and the ability to lift yourself and others up as you move forward in your career—always using your heart, your head, and your grit.

Lisa

1

Sorrow and Self-Doubt
Come Crashing Home

It was Saturday, April 11, 1987. The phone rang at two a.m.

How odd, I thought. *We aren't on call to answer the phones tonight, so who would be calling us this late?*

My husband, Michael, picked it up. He began to cry.

I sat up in our bed, thinking something horrible had happened. I rolled over to his side, and he handed me the receiver. Through his tears, he said, "It's your mom. Your dad is dead."

My subconscious brain said, *No, that just can't be*. But my conscious brain, which was barely awake, realized this must be true.

He was dead. My dad was dead.

I heard myself asking my mom, "What happened?"

She thought it was his heart. She had heard a sound in their hotel room and turned on the light, and Dad was gone, she says.

Not my dad, I said to myself. *On his birthday*.

I started to cry, and I couldn't stop.

My husband and I had just been at the same airport as my parents the night before, and I hadn't even seen them. I'd wanted to find them and say goodbye at their gate—like you could do at that time—but our luggage had been lost and instead we had gone to make a claim. We'd been at the same place, but I missed the chance to say goodbye. And now he was dead, at fifty-three.

So many questions ran through my head: *What do I do now? What does this mean? Who do I call next?*

I wasn't sure of the answer to any of them. Never once in all my eight years as a funeral director had I ever had to tell a person that someone they loved had died. I usually saw people later, after they already knew. *How will I share this news with the people closest to me?* I wondered.

As I floundered inwardly, my mom, being a practical, under-control, logical doctor's daughter, began giving me a list of to-dos, telling me to first call our managers and let them know. She told me to next go—before breakfast—to my grandmother's and tell her, along with my brother Mark. Then, I was to call my younger brother Paul, who was away at college. Mom was packing up their bags and heading to the airport in two hours and had some other calls to make. I was to pick her up in a few hours when she arrived. Oh, and find a funeral home in Nashville.

"Wait," I said, "a funeral home in Nashville, Tennessee? I don't know any. How do I do that? I don't have my funeral home guide-book with me; it's in my office."

Mom suggested I ask our managers, Jim and Dale, or the med-ical examiner.

These words hit me like a rock. Dad was at the medical exam-iner's office?

My dad was in a morgue, and I was just not comprehending how this was all possible right now.

I'd already gone through a full box of tissues. And I began to cry again.

Once I hung up the phone, I slowly rose, walked to the bathroom, and splashed cold water on my face. Somehow, it stopped my crying, and suddenly, I could think straight.

My husband was still in our bedroom sobbing. But I couldn't cry any more right now. It was time to call my managers.

My dad's body was in the morgue in Nashville, and it was my job to get him out of there and bring him home. I was a funeral director. This is what I knew how to do. Time to get back to work.

Yet as much as I was trying to steel myself to do what needed to be done, I was still not entirely sure how to do it. And this was just the beginning of my growing uncertainty and self-doubt, rising alongside my deep, sudden grief.

First, I must figure out how to share this news. It's never easy to tell someone that a person they care about so deeply has died. Having to do this now was a first for me. I knew that Jim and Dale, who had been my dad's managers for decades, would be devastated. What would I say, how would I say it—and all while sitting with my own grief?

I had to tell them, "Dad's dead!" His body ceased to work; his heart gave out. He was never going to come back, to give me his Dave Baue smirky smile, to give me his big dad bear hugs, or to tease me and make me laugh with his corny and sometimes off-color jokes.

I thought how he also wouldn't be here to run the funeral home anymore, and he had promised me he was going to start teaching me things about ownership. I knew nothing about how to run a funeral home business; I was just a funeral director, along with being a young wife and a mother. And also, he now wouldn't be here to watch his four-year-old grandson grow up.

I felt a gamut of emotions run through me. I asked myself, *How will I ever survive in this world without my dad?*

When someone significant dies in your life, the world stops for you. You have no idea how to function. It's like you are holding your breath for a long, long time. You are fearful; you feel paralyzed.

I knew that in that moment, I had to figure it out. Now, it was my job.

Is this what it's like to be "in charge" now? Am I now in charge? I wondered. *Or is it my mother? Or is it Jim and Dale? I'm just a funeral director*, I thought again. *I don't know anything about running a business. How could I possibly ever do it?* Then, I realized that neither did my mother, and unlike me, she'd never even worked at the funeral home.

So many thoughts were popping into my head. I tried to get them under control. *Just make the phone call, Lisa*, I said to myself.

I took a big breath and picked up the phone to dial Jim and Dale—my mentors, my managers, and my friends. Somehow, I shared the news. They told me they were on their way.

I put on a big pot of coffee and headed to the bathroom to take a shower. I knew sleep would not be possible at that point, so it was time to get going.

Within the hour, the doorbell rang. It was Jim and Dale.

It will be okay now, I said to myself. *They will know what to do.*

As they stepped through my front door, I felt myself collapse in their arms, and I started sobbing again. They were crying, too, as they held on to me. But because they were emotionally strong leaders and our managers and they felt they had to, they held it together a little bit better. We slowly walked up the stairs together into my tiny kitchen. As we walked, I realized I was holding a roll of toilet paper and it was leaving a trail behind me. I quickly tried to reroll the toilet paper, embarrassed. We all laughed a little.

Then, we sat down in front of a big box of Kleenex and the three coffee mugs I'd set out. I had already put on another pot of coffee because I'd known we would need a lot of it in the next few hours. We sat, sipped our coffee, blew our noses, and looked at each other in silence. I figured I better speak up, say something, start asking them questions. So I looked at them both and simply said, "What do we do now?"

We began to discuss who would do what next and when. As we sat and drank more coffee, I started making a to-do list, and they started making theirs. I found out that they had no idea whether Dad ever wrote down his prearrangements. I thought they might be somewhere in his office. We also began talking about how we would get Dad back and how to find a funeral home in Nashville. I didn't want Dad to come home in a cardboard shipping container. He was a funeral-home owner; he needed to be in some type of casket on the airplane.

We continued talking arrangements and checking items off our lists. I pulled a funeral file from my briefcase, and as I looked at it, I realized that I must put my dad's name on it. It was another moment when it hit me: He was, indeed . . . dead.

My hand was shaking, and I was not sure I could do this.

I got up to go find a pen and offered to make another pot of coffee. Then, I looked at the table and saw a file with my dad's name on it, which one of my managers had already started.

Of course, I thought. *This is what good funeral directors do: They get organized in advance, even when they are grieving.* And I felt grateful I wasn't the one to have to write his name on a decedent's file.

We kept making lists on our Baue notepads: of people to call, things to do, what each of our jobs would be—what to do next.

I made a little breakfast, and we drank many cups of coffee. We only had a matter of days to plan the largest and most significant funeral we had ever done in our careers.

Eventually, one of them suggested we meet later that morning at the office and start to get things ready for my mom to arrive early afternoon.

We parted ways.

FINDING A WAY THROUGH

Once Jim and Dale arrived at my house that morning, I didn't feel alone anymore. I had my managers; my role models; the men who had trained, mentored, and coached me in the business for the last eight years. We were in this together. We were a team. Teams can accomplish many great things together, especially when using their heads, hearts, and grit.

We each had our gifts that got us through this. At the time, though, I honestly didn't know exactly what my role was or how I could contribute. I was pulled between being a daughter and being a funeral director.

As much as having Jim and Dale there helped me get through the morning, talking with them was also strange in ways. I wondered, *Was I going to be their boss, or were they going to be mine? Was I going to take over the business? Could I possibly do such a thing?*

What will we do now? What will I do now? I asked myself.

Jim and Dale had been with us at Baue's as long as I could remember, all the way from my childhood. They were my teachers and mentors these last eight years. Yet the funeral home was Baue's, and I was the only Baue there right then who was an active funeral director. My mom, even though she had her license, had never really been an active part of the day-to-day operations of the business and didn't want to be a managing owner, ever.

Yet I was just a young woman, all of thirty years old. With my dad's sudden death, one of the biggest anchors in my life had just disappeared, and I felt the weight of the world had dropped onto my shoulders.

I felt fear of the future, fear of the unknown. I didn't know whether the company would continue and we'd all keep our jobs. If it did, would I be the one running it? I didn't know how I could possibly run this funeral home that had, up until then, been "all Dave Baue."

I had never run a company before. I was a Spanish major with a minor in Portuguese. I never went to business school. My dad didn't even want me to go to mortuary school (one of my regrets over the years, but another story for another day).

I was filled with self-doubt. I asked myself, *Will Jim, Dale, and the others support me? Follow me? Help me?*

I have this terrible habit of looking and thinking too far ahead. Some may call it visionary, and at times, it can be, but it's also gotten me in trouble a lot over the years as I've had difficulty focusing in the here and now. It's been a blessing and many times a curse. As I struggled through that first morning after my dad died, I did my best to let these thoughts about the future go and remain grounded in the present.

Yet in that present moment, I also felt incredible grief. The death of a loved one has a way of turning you inside out.

Questions also filled my mind. I wondered, *Why did my dad die out of town? Why on his birthday?*

I did my best, though, to also set these questions aside, at least enough to function. It was time to get to work and help plan my dad's funeral. First, though, I had to do the hardest thing I would do that morning yet: I still had to tell my younger brothers and my grandmother—my father's mother—that Dad was dead.

I braced myself for another impossible task, and, with difficulty, I somehow did it.

After telling my brothers and grandmother, I called my aunts and uncles and let them do the rest. The word was soon out; all our family, staff, friends, and ministers had been contacted. And from there, the phone calls seemed like they never stopped. In 1987, there were no cell phones, only landlines, and they rang constantly on the multiple phone lines both at the house and the office, so much so that getting dressed was nearly impossible. Thank goodness we had long cords on the receivers!

Plus, people were already calling nonstop and showing up at the door, both at home and at the funeral home, with food and flowers. It was getting overwhelming to handle, and it was only the first day. My dad was so well known and loved. And people call and bring food and flowers to provide comfort, as symbols of their love, and as a way to express their sympathies—all good things, but at times, the volume can be overwhelming for families if they don't have help to manage it all. That's what we do as funeral directors: help them. But in our moments of grief, who helps us?

My grandmother always taught me to be a lady who does not go out in public without looking proper and with lipstick on. And so I put on my lipstick (and in true Baue woman fashion, that lipstick stayed on all day). After I was dressed, it was time to head into the office to see whether Dad had written down any of his wishes to give us guidance.

I had my doubts on this, as only a few weeks before he died, I was visiting with him and asked him if he had made his preplans. He turned to me, winked, and said, "Your mother and you kids will know what to do." He did also share that if anything ever happened to him and our mom, he had left a letter in his desk front drawer with some guidelines and suggestions. I would need to look for it.

Hours later, after meeting with our staff and fielding as many phone calls and questions as I could, I stood in my dad's office at his desk looking at his picture and crying. I felt so alone, like the future of the business was in my hands. I had no idea how I was going to sustain it, not mess it up, be able to make it work, or ever—if offered the opportunity—be able to afford to buy it. There was that thinking-ahead thing again. I tried once more to stuff it.

I looked around the room at my dad's black and gold leopard-print wallpaper, his green shag carpet, his gold leather chair. The room smelled like Dad, with his favorite pipe tobacco and his cologne.

My thoughts went to the many times we were in this office together, talking about the progress of the company or how I was doing as a funeral director. I remembered the time I came in to ask him about a raise or the time I had to tell him I buried someone in the wrong vault or backed the hearse into the carriage house and it was out of commission for a week. I missed him so intensely in that moment. He was my role model, my teacher, my mentor, my coach, my dearest daddy. It was hard to believe he would never be back in his office and I would never be able to talk to him again in this room.

I walked to the desk and looked down at the various items in front of me: stacks of files, his notepad and pen, his leather desk set. I hesitantly walked forward and stared at his desk chair, and I felt tears well up in my eyes. I thought to myself, *Do I dare sit in his chair?* As I lowered myself down into it, the tears began to flow again. I felt connected yet somehow overwhelmed, thinking, *I cannot possibly be like my dad, be the leader he was. There is no way.*

After blowing my nose, I straightened up and pulled in closer to his desk.

I felt like I could sense him. There was a real feeling of comfort—like somehow, I could talk to him here. I found myself saying out loud, "Dad, what am I supposed to do now? How will this company survive without you?" Between sniffles, my self-doubt intensified, and I continued. "I don't know how to run a business. I've never done this before. Please help me, tell me what to do, give me a sign. What do I do?"

I began to peek inside his main file drawers, thinking, *Perhaps there is an answer in here.* Maybe I would find some kind of to-do list or checklist of things that could guide me. But there was nothing that gave me an answer.

Then, I remembered the letter. I needed to read that letter.

I pulled out the skinny pencil-and-pen drawer, where he told me he had put it, and immediately saw an envelope addressed to me and my brothers. It said, "Open if your mother and I are gone."

What do I do with this? I thought. Mom was still alive, yet I felt there were some answers for me in the letter. *Did Dad have a premonition that something was going to happen?* I slowly turned the envelope over and over, thinking, *I can't open this. My mom is still alive.* And the letter was not just for me.

I closed my eyes and felt myself pulled in two directions. Should I show it to my mom? Did she know about it? What about my brothers? What did it say? After tussling back and forth, I decided to open the letter. I had asked my dad for a sign, and I felt he had somehow answered and led me here today.

As I slowly opened the envelope, I felt a twinge of guilt. I am a rule follower, not a breaker. And if my dad told me not to do something, I always respected his wishes—at least after I was done with my teenage years. Yet I needed to read this. I picked up my dad's letter opener and broke the envelope open.

At first, it shared what I thought it would say: how much they loved us and would miss us, but they were in a better place, together and happy. They knew we were sad, and they wanted us to know we were going to be okay.

Then, my dad shared his thoughts about the business. He wrote how hard it was, of the deep emotional toll this work could take, and how he did not want the same life for us. He told us to sell it, take the money, and go live our lives. Then, he said we were to call his good friend John Morrow, who worked for a company called Service Corporation International (SCI).

My mind was racing. SCI was a huge corporation. Why would he want us to sell? Was Dad not as happy as he seemed in the business? Did he think it was too stressful for us to handle?

My brother Mark had quit a couple of years ago and gone into acting, saying he didn't like the business. My youngest brother, Paul, was still in college—who knew what he wanted to do yet? Then, I thought, *Wait a minute. What about me?* I was already in the business, and Dad thought we should still sell it? My inner voice of self-doubt roared louder as I thought, *Maybe Dad didn't think I could handle being an owner.* I knew I wasn't ready, but didn't he want to give me a chance? I wondered whether perhaps he wrote this before I was even at the funeral home.

I looked for a date on the letter, and it wasn't there. *Hmmm,* I said to myself. Maybe this was written some time ago, when he didn't think I was ready or experienced enough yet. *Yes, that must have been it,* I said to myself. *He wrote this many years ago.* After all, I had only been licensed for eight years.

I was sure that was it. At least that's what I had to believe.

All I knew was how to be a funeral director. I didn't know how to run a business, manage people, or handle the financial side of things. Yet while I knew I had a lot to learn, I wanted the challenge. I wanted to step into the new role. *We have good managers,* I thought. *A good accountant. We will be okay, and they can teach me. Gosh, I hope they want to.*

My mind was swirling. I thought about my trip to Houston just the week prior to visit SCI's corporate headquarters, where I spent time with John Morrow, the VP of the company and a dear friend of my parents. I thought of my dad's hope for a different life for us kids, and I also thought of what I wanted. I thought of what I could do with hard work and the powerful mentors in my life. I thought of what I should now do with this letter.

I sat in contemplation for a few minutes. Then, there was a knock on the door that brought me quickly out of my thoughts and into reality. Mom and my brothers were here, and it was time to go downstairs to make funeral arrangements. Dad had just died yesterday, and I did my best to ground myself in today's reality. No decisions on the future of the business needed to be made then. I quickly stuck the letter in my purse and headed out the door.

THE RIGHT SUPPORT MEANS EVERYTHING

My mom wanted to plan everything quickly; there was no slowing her down. It was a very strange feeling, being on the other side of the table as a daughter who was mourning. As I watched her, calm, composed, with her makeup and well-styled hair and not a tear in her eye, I thought, *How is she doing this?* She seemed to know exactly what to do, what he would have wanted, and what she wanted too. I just wanted to cry and cry.

My dad hadn't written down his prearrangements, so we as a family did what we thought was best. We knew the visitation and funeral would be a huge and exhausting event, and my mom wanted more than two days of public viewing. Planning went by in a blur, my mom doing most of the decision-making, my one brother crying most of the time, and the other looking like he was far away in another world. I was just deeply sad, yet I tried to engage in the process and help my mom figure out logistics, along with selections of services and products. I really didn't feel like picking out a casket or flowers or songs for a ceremony, but I knew it was necessary. I was already leaning into at least an attempt to use my head, my heart, and the deep grit—or, in other words, the courage and determination to persevere—that had been taught to and instilled in me from my earlier years.

After the arrangements were complete, Mom sent us all home to get our clothes and items ready for the next day. We were to have a two-day visitation, with the funeral on the third day. This may seem overwhelming to some today; however, in 1987, it was a tradition to have a full one- or two-day visitation before the funeral occurred, especially when someone of prominence died. Now, visitations and family time with their deceased loved ones are more likely to last for a few hours at most. With the sudden shock of Dad dying so suddenly, though, anything less than three days would not have been enough time for us to process and accept his death. In fact, I felt like I needed more time than I had. My mom's sense of urgency was in high gear to "get it over with quickly," and although I know this is normal when there is extreme emotional pain, taking more time before services occurred would have helped us integrate the shock.

There was so much to mourn, it would take a long time. Thankfully, the visitation helped us begin to do so as well as we could.

Over the next two days, there had to be more than three thousand people who came through the funeral home. As overwhelming as that may seem to some, it was a great deal of comfort for all of us. We had a chance to meet so many people my dad cared for and supported over the years. Numerous members of our community and professional friends both locally and from out of state came to pay their respects and share their Dave Baue stories, many of which we had never heard. Each and every one of them offered words of comfort and gave us hugs.

The family therapist Virginia Satir said, "We need four hugs a day for survival. We need eight hugs a day for maintenance. We need twelve hugs a day for growth." During the visitation, my "hug cup" overflowed, and I felt the love of the community that so loved my dad. It was healing. If we had shortened the visitation or not had one at all, we would neither have had this experience or this comfort nor felt all this love that surrounded us. I was finding much-needed comfort while I also sat with incredible sadness, my uncertainty, and my questions about the future.

In the middle of this overwhelming experience, one of my staff members found me to tell me there was someone on the phone trying to reach me. I thought, *Can't I call them back? Surely it can wait.* But they insisted on speaking to me right then.

As I walked back to the hallway and our flower delivery room to answer the phone in a quiet private area, I wondered who it could be and why it was so urgent.

When I said hello, I tried my best to put on a nice, pleasant voice. The voice on the other end of the line turned out to be an instructor from the Women in Funeral Service Conference whom I had met a couple of years before. She was a good friend of my dad's and an owner of her own firm as well.

After she shared her sympathies and we shared a few tears together, she next asked, "Lisa, what will you do now about the business?"

I was taken aback, thinking to myself, *Now? I am just trying to get through my dad's visitation and funeral. I am not prepared to have this conversation today.*

Yet we were having it. I shared with her both my desire to step into this role and my self-doubts.

In response, she shared her belief in me, that I was a smart young woman and I could absolutely run, own, and manage this business. She told me she would help and support me on this journey and that in the next few weeks, I needed to declare my intentions of learning how to become an owner of the business to my mom. I protested, saying that seemed a bit soon, but she replied that no, the time was now. "You can do this, Lisa," she said. "I will help you and mentor you."

As I walked away and slowly returned to the visitation, I felt a dawning sense of peace. I now had the support I needed to forge forward with what I knew I wanted. I now had the support of a confident, successful female owner who would help me.

Self-Reflection Questions

- How has the death of a dear friend or family member affected you in your life and career? How did you seek help for your grief?

- Describe a time when you have experienced serious self-doubt. What do you remember most clearly about the experience?

- How do you make time to take care of yourself, even when work is busy (or hard)?

- How have you developed a support network of mentors to turn to in times of need?

2

The Power of Grit
and Early Mentors

The days after my dad's funeral were a bit of a blur. As a family, we tried our best to normalize. My managers told me to take the rest of the week—even a couple of weeks—off. *But how is that possible?* I asked myself. I needed to go in and help, find out what I was supposed to do next. Within a day or two, I was back in the office, hanging with the Baue team. Just being back in a routine gave me a feeling of normalcy. And being there with everyone gave me comfort and maybe helped them a little too.

Sitting still and doing nothing were, and are, painful for me. I needed to take some action, and I didn't know what that looked like other than to put on my navy pinstriped funeral suit and gold Baue "B" lapel pin and drive into the office. My heart had been shattered, and at the same time, I needed to make some decisions.

When I first learned of my father's death and questioned what would happen next, I had been overwhelmed with self-doubt. Could I really become an owner and buy the company? But with the phone call at my dad's visitation and the words of the woman owner who would go on to become one of my first female mentors,

I was starting to believe in myself. I could do it, with the right help. And I knew I wanted to at least give it a try.

It was time to talk with my mom.

THE RIDER IS ALWAYS IN CHARGE

Before the visit, my self-doubt continued to whisper and roar. What would I say to her? Would she think I could manage our company? Did I even really think so? As mixed feelings and thoughts churned in my head, I heard my grandfather's voice in my ear: "It will be okay, Lisa. I taught you to be tough and have grit. When life knocks you down, when you get bucked off that pony, you get right back on it and show them that you can be a good boss. You are strong and resilient. You can do this."

My mind drifted back to my childhood years and my times with my grandfather, Arthur Baue, who founded our company in 1935. Pop, as we grandchildren called him, grew up very poor on a small farm and had lived through the Depression. He taught me so many lessons in being resilient when I was with him as a child visiting him and my grandma at their summer vacation home, a working farm in southern Illinois. One of my first lessons came from two Shetland ponies appropriately named Thunder and Lightning.

The farm had all the animals most working farms did: chickens, pigs, milk cows, beef cattle, and a horse or two. Pop decided that as his number of grandchildren grew, we needed ponies for the younger ones. I was the oldest and an avid horse rider and lover, so naturally, it was my job to help my younger cousins ride when they came to visit. It was also my job to help get the ponies fit for riding each spring. What I hadn't realized that first summer after the ponies arrived is that they needed to be broken in after the winter—and that would be my job, too.

I remember sitting on top of these little mini-horses, my feet almost touching the ground, my hands on the tiny saddle horn, and hearing my grandfather say, "hold on" and "giddyup" as he cracked the whip on the ground behind one of the ponies. I didn't last long in the saddle as the pony bucked and reared in protest. As I picked myself up off the dusty ground, spat the dirt out of my mouth, and picked the grass out of my hair, my grandfather said, "Now, get back on that pony, girl, and show them who's boss."

And I did. Over and over again.

The breaking of the ponies went on for at least an hour or more (it seemed like all day), until they were finally rideable, walking and trotting without bucking. As I slowly walked with a little limp in one foot back to the farmhouse to get cleaned up, my grandfather gave me a pat on the back and said I had done a good job that day. He told me to remember: The rider is always in charge and the boss of the horse. He also said horses sense fear and advised me to never let them feel it from me, ever.

That lesson had stayed with me through my childhood and into adulthood. When things got tough, I always got back on the pony. And as I heard his voice in my ear now, as I readied myself to talk with my mom about the future of the business, I lifted myself up once more. *But still*, I wondered, *can I convince my mom I can be in charge?* There was so much I didn't know: how to manage people; how to manage a business; how to understand things like financials, pricing, HR, legal and compliance issues. It all felt overwhelming.

Then, I remembered the support and help from my managers on the morning of Dad's death. I remembered the teamwork that allowed us to plan a meaningful and life-honoring event for my dad, one that would remain in my heart and the hearts of our family, staff, and community for years to come. *Yes*, I said to myself, *that is the answer: teamwork*. It all did feel overwhelming, but I knew with the right help and mentoring, I could learn. Together, we could do this.

As the day of the talk approached, our manager Dale, who knew my intentions and desire to learn to lead the business, shared that he was willing to come with me to meet with my mom. I was grateful. I also learned from Dale that my dad had wanted him to become our new general manager, but it had not yet been announced. As he shared this with me, I realized that he wanted to support me in working toward one day buying the business. It seemed none of our future roles were clear, and we needed my mom's help to make these decisions, because she was now the sole owner and decision-maker.

When we sat down at her house, Dale led the conversation. He knew that with my mom, there was no point in beating around the bush. So he came straight out with it and said, "I'm here to ask who you want to oversee the company and manage it going forward."

My mom first validated what Dale had told me earlier: that my dad had wanted him to take over the general manager position. She went on to say that she had no desire to be involved in the day-to-day running of the business. After her announcement, Dale said he felt I should be named head of the company and be given the opportunity to purchase the business as I proved myself, which would give our staff and community assurances that the family business would continue under a Baue. He also shared that he would be there, along with the rest of the staff, to support and train me during my learning and on my path to ownership.

I did not know this was coming and just looked at him in surprise! He really believed in me. My eyes were overwhelmed with tears, and I shook my head—not to disagree, but in disbelief. He believed in me when I didn't believe in myself. Feelings of surprise, relief, and deep gratitude filled me as I looked at him and thanked him for saying this. I knew then that he had my back and always would.

He looked at me, then at my mom, and said, "We will all stand behind her, help her, teach her. She can do it. We all truly believe this." We hugged, and he then gave my mom and me some time alone.

My mom then dropped a surprising comment. "Lisa," she said, "this business killed your dad. I don't want it to do the same to you." *Wow*, I thought, *about the same message as in the letter.* I took the letter out, shared it with her, and asked her whether she knew about it and what it meant.

This opened the discussion further into how difficult the business had been for my dad: how hard it was for him to be around death all the time and how it affected his physical and mental well-being. As I listened to her, I was thinking how it didn't have the same effect on me. It didn't seem to wear me down emotionally. Except for some of the babies and little children who died, I had been able to handle just about every kind of death we experienced, even the horrific ones—the fires, the accidents, the suicides, the murders. I thought maybe I was built differently from my dad; maybe I was more like my mom inside, a doctor and nurse's daughter who cared for others but was able to do it without fully taking on their grief and mourning. Or maybe I was more like my Pop Baue, a tough former farmer who could train the buck out of Shetland ponies. *Maybe my dad couldn't do that*, I thought.

As the discussion continued, I assured my mom I felt able to cope with the death that was a part of our profession. I also shared that I knew I had much to learn from people both inside and outside our company. We agreed to meet again for more discussions about ownership.

Soon after, my mom told me my dad's friends, a group of funeral-home owners, would be gathering together for their annual study group meeting and she had asked them if we could attend. *Me, go to Dad's owners' group?* I thought. *What does this mean? Does she think I can become an owner?* I heard the voice of self-doubt rise again, along with my feelings of grief. I had just buried my dad two short weeks ago; could I do all of this right now?

Then, I heard Pop Baue's voice again: "Lisa, it's going to be okay. You can do this. You are a Baue!" I thought of getting back up on that pony and knew that even through the hard work of grief and the feelings of self-doubt, I had the grit to do this.

ESSENTIAL MENTORSHIP

The meeting with the owners' group was barely two weeks away. I asked my mom what I needed to do to prepare. Her answer was so hilarious to me, I almost laughed out loud.

"Well, Lisa," she said, "the first thing we are going to do is take you shopping for new appropriate resort wear and evening dress-up clothes."

I soon began to realize I was entering a new world: a world where I had to wear more than a funeral suit to work, a world where there would be no more going out in public in my blue jeans and T-shirts or sweatpants on my days off. My mom was telling me that it was time to learn to dress like a leader and a lady. So off we went to buy the clothes that would make this possible.

The next thing I knew, I was trying on dresses (which are not my favorite), nice slacks, blouses, sweaters, and shoes. I am more than six feet tall, with a thirty-six-inch inseam, and in 1987, finding pants and clothing that fit my tall lanky body was a challenge. Our shopping spree took all day, and after what was an exhausting mission, at least for me, we headed to the seamstress to have the pants and jacket sleeves lengthened.

I followed up the shopping day with a trip to the office to see my managers. I learned that all our company reports had been sent to the members of the owners' study group. Up until then, I had never seen these reports and had no clue what they were or how to understand them. I didn't even know whether our company made much money or if it was profitable.

I was grateful for the patience my managers and accountant had with me that week as they began to go over the reports with me and I tried to learn. I probably asked the same questions repeatedly each time we met. Finally, though, before my mom and I left for the meeting, I felt I had a small understanding of the business management reports, what they meant, and a little working knowledge of the company operations.

We left for Sea Island, Georgia. My crash course in funeral-home ownership was about to begin. I was grateful to have my mom with me at the first part of the meeting as I would have to sit in a room full of my dad's contemporaries, all men, who had owned their own businesses for twenty to thirty years. My mom reassured me it would all be fine.

The week began with a cocktail party and dress-up dinner in the dining room of the Cloisters resort, a place where many US presidents vacationed. My insecurity and image button were on high alert, and I probably redid my hair and makeup three times that first day. (Thank goodness my mom had taken me shopping.)

As the days went on, I relaxed a bit more. The owners, who had been friends with my dad for years, were kind and understanding, and I soon realized I had a whole new group of mentors. These men became like uncles to me, as well as long-term supporters.

During this week of meetings, they helped me understand more about the condition of our business. And not all of this was the most positive of news, especially when it came to the new business my dad had just finished acquiring from his business partner: the cemetery.

Now, I had another question: Would I buy the cemetery business as well?

Few of the study group members had cemeteries. In fact, back in the late 1980s, cemeteries were seen as competitors to funeral homes. Regardless, I asked one of the financially astute members to help me review the cemetery financial statements and balance sheets.

What we found in them was worrisome. The cemetery was not in good financial shape, and, in fact, it had a great deal of debt to the former owner, along with excessive liabilities. The cemetery was not cash flowing. None of this was known to me until after Dad died and I attended this first study group meeting. Initially, I did not understand how the transaction affected the business overall.

I learned that the study group members did not think most funeral-home owners made good cemetery owners. This reflected wider opinion within the profession; in fact, on a national level back in the '80s, funeral-home owners and cemetery owners did not see eye to eye in business best practices, legislative matters, and sales techniques. (In many instances today, they still do not.)

Since I was coming in green and knew nothing about running a cemetery, I didn't really understand these common conflicts and how we could better serve our client families with both companies. Conducting a funeral and arranging a burial draws upon a different skill set than what is, in essence, selling burial products in advance.

On top of this, the company seemed to be using today's money to pay for yesterday's liabilities; it had little savings and profit margins at the time. What was I going to do with it? Yet it seemed a natural extension of what a funeral home company did, and it was in an ideal location for a nice funeral home to be built in the future. It could be a positive addition to the business . . . if I could find the financing.

In that year when I was preparing to buy the funeral home,

after much consultation with my study group mentors and other financial experts, I declined to buy the cemetery without a new appraisal. In a new appraisal, the liabilities and debt would be taken into account for a much reduced and more affordable price. (When I did later agree to purchase it, I insured the former owner, and I insured my mom, a fifty-year-old, two-pack-a-day smoker. Imagine the premiums!)

My mentors helped me navigate this new territory. For decades to come, they continued to be there for me as a reliable, trusted resource, men who always answered the phone when I called with questions ranging from understanding financials to dealing with bankers, accountants, attorneys, regulators, and everything in between.

Learning to understand the funeral business as a business was not easy for me. I didn't initially have the confidence in myself that I could do the necessary math, manage cash flow, and understand things like complicated financial statements, balance sheets, depreciated assets, and debt-to-equity ratios. I never loved math when I was in school, and I had no background in finance or accounting. I was a Spanish major with a minor in Portuguese who had planned to be a travel agent. Now, here I was with a funeral and cemetery business to run. However, I knew it was important to prove I could learn to do it, so I worked hard to study and learn these aspects of owning and operating a business. I learned a great deal about budgeting and long-term debt from studying the historical information on past years of the business. This turned out to be an essential lesson, because I would need to take on a great deal of debt in order to purchase the business from my mom.

I never could have learned all of this alone. Although my husband at the time had a sharp financial mind and worked in the funeral service profession, he was then working for another company. I was undertaking this mission to learn and become an owner independently. I'm thankful for the support of my mom as she pointed me toward the right people who could help me. These study group mentors made all the difference.

I came to enjoy what I was learning. Studying finances took time, and it was hard but not impossible. It was the work that owners do all the time, and so could I. As I learned, I would take out my highlighter and look at variances (differences) in the financials from year to year. I asked others to compile them into graphs, charts, and comparison sheets. Now, I could really see the problems—and some of the solutions, too. This actually became fun. I loved to look at these kinds of reports, sitting in group meetings with my owner friends and talking about new strategies to make the business better and more profitable.

As the years went by, the financial news was not always good. Sometimes, the death rate wavered and went backwards, and we had overestimated our income in our budgeting. Sometimes, the task of paying down the debt seemed overwhelming. I realized that to be a business owner, you must have or develop the ability to use your head and, many times, make tough financial decisions. You must have thick skin and perseverance—the drive to push through, which I call grit. My Pop Baue first taught me to develop it, and it grew stronger in me over the years.

My dad was a huge John Wayne fan, and *True Grit* was one of my favorite John Wayne films we watched together. During the difficult times in the business, it reminded me of the movie's heroine, Mattie Ross, lying in a snake pit. I was learning more and more that when times get tough, you do your best to survive and learn from them.

I was also learning that when you don't know what to do, you can't just rely on yourself; you reach out and ask others stronger, smarter, and wiser than you for advice and help.

Some people fear that asking for help is a weakness and that asking questions will cause others to see them in a poor light. I overcame that fear rather quickly as a young adult, because I felt I had a responsibility to the company, the Baue team, and the community to become a questioner and a lifelong learner, to understand the good, the bad, and the ugly of operating a business. I am sure I drove our managers; our in-house accountant, Larry; my dad's friends; and my mentors crazy back then with all my questions. I'll be forever grateful for their patience with me and the many years of dedication, loyalty, and teaching they gave to me as a potential future and eventually current owner.

THE PATH TO OWNERSHIP

I spent the first two years after Dad's death absorbing all I could, learning the facts and figures and reaching out to others to learn what I needed to do to run a successful business. The next spring, I was asked to come back to the owners study group in Sea Island, Georgia, as a guest. I was excited to return and felt much better prepared to speak about our family business and how it was doing. I felt I was gaining a good grasp on the basics of funeral-home ownership and management.

This second-year meeting was much like the one the year before, except there was a new guest along with me. It was a guy from the Denver area who had just bought his first funeral home, and unlike the other eight older men in the group, he was my age. After hearing his story and learning how he came to be an owner, I was impressed with his work ethic, intelligence, and witty yet sometimes odd sense of humor. In funeral service, where you're exposed to death day in and day out, having fun and being able to bring humor into your career are imperative. His name was John Horan.

We bonded immediately. We were the youngest in the group that year and were both guests. Here was a guy I thought I could be life-long friends with, learn from, and grow up with in the profession in the years to come. And that is exactly what happened.

I don't know if it was based on the strength of my presentation, the fact I'd done my homework and knew my business numbers, or my charming personality (LOL), but that year, I was asked to join the study group, along with my new friend John. The group asked me to join during a long walk down the beach after one of our meetings. I remember one of my dad's best friends asking me on that walk if I would rather be in an owners group with people my own age. What was funny to me then, and still today, is that my friend John and I were only thirty-eight days apart in age and he was also being asked to join the group that year without perhaps getting that question, too. When I mentioned that fact in response, the man who asked me the question raised his eyebrows a bit, and then a smile came to his face, followed by a big laugh. I am pretty sure I was really being asked whether I, as a woman, wanted to join a group of all men or whether I'd prefer to instead find a group of owners more like me, composed of mostly women. In reality, there were no women owners in funeral service study groups at that time, and to this day, they still only exist in small numbers in our profession.

Regardless of gender differences, I found the owners study group to be an excellent space for mentorship, and our integration of various demographics and personalities is part of what allowed for such a dynamic exchange of ideas. I highly recommend joining a group like this to better learn business best practices and create lifelong friendships.

Many of these older men remained mentors and friends of mine throughout the years. From the day we met until the day they retired, I would see them at various meetings and conventions, along with sharing our times together in the study group. Their wise counsel has stayed with me throughout my years as an owner. Without this owners study group to help me grow up, gain confidence in my abilities, and teach me how to run a funeral business, I would have surely failed.

Over the course of these first few years after my dad died, I learned so much. It was the knowledge that I needed to begin to manage a funeral-home business. I did it while still grieving the man who had come before me, my beloved dad. I had to find space to hold it all, hold the grief and memory of my dad, while also moving forward—in my life and with the business as Lisa Baue, owner. I had to be strong and my own type of owner, bringing my sense of style and ideas to the company.

During the first two years after my dad's death, I realized that sitting at my dad's desk just didn't feel right, so instead, I shared an office with our grief counselor on staff at that time. Based on our conversations, I knew I had to eventually make some changes, claim the space, and bring in my personality, preferences, and style. Dad had loved his office, and so a big part of me didn't want to change it. But the masculine colors, big walnut desk, green shag carpet, and animal print just weren't me. I knew deep down I needed the office to feel like it was my own space. I knew I needed to create a place that was peaceful, with colors that made me feel calm and gave me confidence. I needed to have a room where I could have the privacy and space I needed to learn.

Once I was able to remodel, I found some neutral carpet, changed out the desk (giving Dad's desk to one of our managers), and put in some whites, beiges, light greens, and soft pinks. It became a comfortable place for me to read, think, learn, and have private meetings. I was moving forward and settling into my own space and my new role as the future owner.

I had the support of team Baue, especially my managers and my mom, and in my third year, I felt it was time to figure out how to finance the purchase of the family business. I didn't know exactly what it was worth, although I knew I would be taking on at least $2 million in debt or more. Back in 1989 that was more money than I could even fathom possible. I had no idea how I would ever find enough money to afford it. Yet I knew I wanted to and had to.

So once again, I reached out to my mentors for help. I went to my mom and told her I felt I was ready to make a commitment to become an owner. I talked to her legal counsel, her accountant, the banks, and my owners study group. I was very fortunate that a stock value formula had been established at the time of my dad's death and estate settlement. It was a combination of EBITDA (earnings before interest, taxes, depreciation, and amortization) along with a formula that established the price per case (i.e., per death call).

The financial audit began after my dad's estate was settled and the purchase price was established. When the price was presented to me, I thought, *There is no way I can afford this.* I was a mom of a six-and-a-half-year-old, my savings were slim, and my husband and I were just making enough to pay our bills, set aside some in our retirement account, and maybe take a weeklong vacation once a year, but it was usually to our family lake house or combined with a funeral convention.

My self-doubt and fears kicked in again. How could I possibly afford this? I needed help. Maybe I needed a partner who had more financial knowledge than I did. Even though I had studied the finances for the last two-and-a-half years, I still did not have the confidence in myself that I could do this alone. What was I going to do? How could I make this business purchase work and still make a living? Could the business and I afford this long-term debt? I thought again about my dad's letter. Would buying the business cause me regret? Would it be too much stress to have this much debt? The thought of it was really scary.

It was then that Pop Baue's voice came back again to me to rely on my toughness and resiliency—my grit: "You can do it, Lisa." I also remembered the words from my first female mentor: "I believe in you. I will be here for you. I will support you."

With my mom holding the note and the bank financing, I was able to afford the debt. Of course, the company, its assets, its buildings, and its receivables were tied up as collateral. I had to personally guarantee all the debt, as did my mom. I will be forever grateful to her for believing in me and for the help, loyalty, wise counsel, and belief of the Baue managers, my study group, and my mentors.

It would take time before I came to believe in myself the same way.

I set off on a new chapter of my life as a funeral-home owner with more than $2.5 million in debt and working to turn an upside-down cemetery around so I could eventually buy it too.

Piece of cake, right?

Continuing to draw upon my grit, my head, and the guidance of my mentors and advisors would be enough to see me through. Or so I thought.

Self-Reflection Questions

- Do you enjoy working on the business side of things? Please share some of your favorite areas that you enjoy most.

- Do you understand the essential principles of business and finance as well as you would like to? If not, what goals do you have to learn more?

- What lessons have you learned from people who were unlike you in some important way (e.g., age or gender)?

- Are you part of a professional peer study group? Would you like to be? What would you most like to learn from one?

3

Finding My Place
in a Man's World

After purchasing the business, I continued to learn. And it wasn't always about how to read financials and run a death-care company. It was often about how to best claim my space in a male-dominated world as a woman. In some areas, I thrived. In others, I still struggled and did not feel as competent. Sitting in a room full of men at every meeting I attended felt very intimidating. They seemed so intelligent and confident, and I didn't feel I was as smart; after all, I was only a funeral director and a Spanish major. So mostly, I remained quiet. I listened and I learned. I also felt a bit overwhelmed at times. I wondered how and whether I could ever get to a place where I could be like them yet still be myself.

This feeling I had when I was in the big convention meetings with mostly, if not all, men was one that caused me to have a little fear of speaking up. I wasn't sure that I had anything to contribute, and I wanted to be accepted and respected but also not seen as trying too hard. I also realized that learning takes time, and I had a great deal to learn, both professionally and in how I acted within the group.

FITTING IN

Soon, I knew sitting in on meetings with them was not enough. The more I thought about it, the more I realized that friendships were important, too, so I set out to join as many groups and participate in as many activities as I could to be accepted as "one of the boys." This may or may not seem to some to be the right way to approach things, but back in the '80s and '90s, for me, it seemed to work.

My study group was a big part of what helped me learn to become accepted as one of the few licensed women owners in our profession. In my time with these supportive male friends and mentors, I learned how to fit in and hold my own as "one of the guys." As I settled into our friendships, I felt I could be myself with them. I did not have to be the acceptable "polite" lady at all times. They were my contemporaries and were becoming my best professional buddies. I could let it go, debate an issue in our meetings, and, yes, occasionally use an off-color word.

Spending more and more time in the company of my owners study group and with some of their extended friends allowed me to branch out a bit, get to know other owners and leaders in the profession, and do so in settings that were nontraditional.

As part of this, I was invited to go pheasant hunting with a group of funeral-home owners and professionals. I had shot guns before and killed a few small animals, such as squirrels and rabbits, on my grandfather's farm. Yet I had never been on a formal "guys" hunting trip. My dad, grandfathers, and brothers hunted, but I never went, because it was always an all-guys trip. I often wondered why. My mom, however, was a crack shot at trap and skeet, so over the years, she took me to the range, and I learned to handle a shotgun relatively proficiently.

The first trip pheasant hunting in the rolling hills and cornfields of South Dakota was an eye-opening experience. We stayed in marginally clean hotels, got up at the crack of dawn, put on our orange vests and hats, and prepared for the trip to walk the fields of Native American land.

I was so excited for that first trip with the other owners. I went to an outfitter store and bought new hunting boots, which I was very proud of. What I didn't realize was that they needed to be broken in. After the first day of walking the fields, I ended up with huge blisters on my heels. They were painful and peeling, and no number of Band-Aids or medicine was going to heal them quickly. So being the Baue I was raised to be, I drew on my grit, put my chin up, didn't let the pain show, walked with a slight limp, and went back into the fields the next day and the next. I had been taught to never give up; you keep walking, no matter what the pain, and that's just what I did, with no complaining.

I shot a few pheasants that year, and over the years, I contributed to the group with my shooting. I was forever grateful during these trips to my grandfather Baue, who had taught me the lessons to keep going, even in the face of painful experiences. Showing this confidence, my determination to be better, and a desire to learn from my guy peers gained the group's respect. Each of the men had a nickname they received on their first trip, and I earned one, too: Bad Boots Baue. To this day, they still on occasion use this nickname endearingly—not because I was a bad shot, but because I had earned my badge as field hunter from the four-inch blisters I had on both of my heels from the inside of my boots!

The scuba divers study group I joined a few years later was similar. It was made up of all men, who would work in the mornings, dive in the afternoon, and party, drink, and smoke cigars late into the night, often for periods of several days in a row. I came home from my time with them exhilarated, more knowledgeable, and exhausted, knowing that even though I was in the minority, I found ways to connect with them and eventually gain their respect.

BEING A WOMAN IN A MAN'S WORLD

On the other side of acceptance from the men were the women. I knew it was also important to become friends with their wives and allow my feminine side to be present in our conversations. Some of the wives I met over the years were part of the family business, and some were not. As I spent more time out with my friends and their wives, I learned that social dinners were not time for business talk. I found that conversations needed to be more about our lives personally, and so I shared more about being a wife and mother. Discovering others' interests and joys was a good way to make new friends in this sphere, and in sharing some of my own, I feel I gained some respect as well.

I was grateful for my mother's early lessons. We called her Emily Post the Second because she taught us table manners, the dos and don'ts of dressing, and how to behave as ladies. My mom, Jill, was a very beautiful and feminine woman who had spent her life trying to turn me into a girly girl even though it just wasn't part of who I was inside. However, during times when I was with my friends' wives, these lessons became invaluable.

My grandmother Viola—Vi, or Nana Baue, as we called her— also taught me how to cook and take over the process in the kitchen while still looking and acting like a lady. Except on the farm, Nana Baue always had her hair and nails perfectly done, with her lipstick and earrings on. She donned an apron over her clothes, set a beautiful table, and conducted herself always as a lady. As a kid, I couldn't care less about appearances, but I learned that in our family, they did matter. I was taught that dressing as a lady was important and was told if people didn't respect you, they wouldn't use your company when they died.

Nana was known as the "white-glove lady" by our staff over the years. She was a very particular woman who wanted everything just perfect. She would come into the funeral home from time to time after she retired, and no matter how clean we thought our facilities were, Nana would find dust, cobwebs, or a light out.

Her home was immaculate and beautifully decorated, just as she was. Toward the end of her life, she fell and broke her hip. She spent the night in her garage wrapped only in her bathrobe. My dad was with her in the ER and called me at the funeral home that morning, sharing that I needed to go to Nana's home to get some personal items quickly. She refused to see the doctor until she had her hair brushed and her lipstick on. She never went out in public without her lipstick on and her hair perfectly styled.

I have become the same way as Nana in many ways. As much as I am a tomboy, I value dressing nicely and generally always have my hair and makeup fixed and lipstick on before going out in public. These were the lessons I learned from her and my mom that would serve me into adulthood.

My mother always told me a lady never sweats; she glows. I am not sure whether I ever glowed, especially around my guy friends. Yet I do believe that, over time, I came to be accepted and respected by most of them. It came from not just "becoming" one of the guys but by being resilient and gritty, showing I had much to learn from them, learning to interact and befriend their wives as well, and proving I had the intelligence, professionalism, and inner strength to work and play hard with them, as well as run and grow a successful business in our profession.

My dad had been insistent that I become active in the community and join organizations, so I did. Back in the late '70s and early

'80s, there were segregated organizations in various civic organizations. Mostly men were involved in the chamber of commerce. My entry into the men's world had some ups and downs in our local community.

I joined the Business and Professional Women's Club and the St. Charles Jaycee Women. I learned a great deal from all the women in both of these clubs, had fun, and found friendships that would last a lifetime as we raised our babies together and raised money for community betterment projects. I also learned leadership lessons. Many of these women who were older than me had already paid their dues. They were bankers, principals, owners, and partners with their husbands in various businesses—very smart and hard-working women. I listened to their stories and learned from them how to better integrate into a man's world by finding ways to balance our femininity along with our desire to be respected and accepted for our brains and abilities, using our heads and our hearts! I really enjoyed the women-only groups back then because they were emotionally supportive, helped me feel accepted as a businesswoman, and were encouraging in their advice to me. They were the place to be as a businesswoman in my early years, and looking back, I miss many of the times I shared then with my women friends who brought their listening ears and caring hearts into conversations when I was seeking advice.

Then, in July of 1984, the Supreme Court ruling came about. It was about three years before my dad died. In *Roberts v. US Jaycees*, 468 US 609, it was ruled that the Jaycees civic organization was a public accommodation and could no longer discriminate in its primary membership. At the time, I was a Jaycee woman—a member of their auxiliary women's group—and our organization was dissolved under the National Jaycee Charter. Other civic organizations, such as Rotary, Kiwanis, and Optimists, followed a few years later. After my dad died, I was approached by his Rotary Club to become one of five women chosen to join.

Previously, there had been no women in Rotary, so they formed a committee to change this. I later found out that many of the younger men objected to adding us, but the Supreme Court ruling was pretty clear, and Rotary and other clubs knew it was headed that way, so they reluctantly conformed. As women, we knew we had a lot to prove to be more accepted by our own male peers.

At the time, very few women owned or managed businesses in our St. Charles, Missouri, community. I was asked to join along with our city's first woman mayor, a past Chamber of Commerce president, an attorney, and another small business owner like me.

I remember our first meeting. As the five of us walked in together to be installed, in this room full of more than ninety men, it was a proud moment yet also felt very strange. Yet over time, it became a comfortable place where we were welcomed and accepted as we volunteered for leadership positions and hard work on various fundraisers, such as working the hot-dog stands in the hot, muggy summer. We knew the five of us had to prove ourselves to be accepted. We had to bring humble leadership skills into all we did, and we had to become learners from our older and same-age male peers, showing them respect. At times, that proved difficult because there were many strong male egos in our club who we knew did not want us to be there. It took time, but eventually, we formed lifetime friendships with these men. Many were attorneys, bankers, mayors, police and fire chiefs, and wealthy businessmen. I not only had friends over the years who had my back; I took care of their loved ones' funerals and eventually many of theirs. It was an honor to serve them during those difficult times.

These relationships were incredibly rewarding and personally enriching while also helping me grow as a leader and helping my business grow. They also took work. Seeking to become accepted in a male group and a man's world is never easy for women. It was not easy then, and it is still not easy now. On a state and national level, our profession was, and still is, male dominated, and if you look at the majority of the state and national associations and their boards today, although it is slowly changing, it is still composed of about 70 percent men.

Most organizations today have had at least one or two female board members or presidents in the last ten years, but as of this book's writing, the National Funeral Directors Association (NFDA), founded in 1882, has yet to have a woman elected to the president's position. According to Christine Pepper, NFDA's current CEO, they've had only seven women serve on its board of directors in the history of the organization (despite its staff currently being 72 percent female and 28 percent male). Furthermore, based on NFDA member makeup survey data from 2024, 76 percent of members are male, and 24 percent are female. Of the owners in that group, 83 percent are male, and 17 percent are female, and of the managers in that group, 76 percent are male, and 24 percent are female.[1] Like most of the other associations serving our profession, it is changing, but it is a very slow change.

This lack of equal representation goes well beyond our profession. A report by S&P Global Market Intelligence found that in 2023, women held just 11.8 percent of the C-suite roles assessed.[2] And this imbalance extends into our politics as well. The United States has yet to have a woman president, which has always puzzled

---

[1]   Statistics provided by Christine Pepper, CEO of National Funeral Directors Association. Used with permission.

[2]   Jeanne Sahadi, "Share of Women in C-Suite Roles Falls for First Time in Two Decades, Study Finds," CNN.com, updated April 5, 2024, https://www.cnn.com/2024/04/05/success/gender-parity-women-corporate-leaders/index.html.

me for a country that has been around since 1776, is seemingly progressive, and, since August 1920, has put into place a woman's right to vote (unless you were a Black woman, who, depending on the state, could not vote or take office until 1965, when Lyndon B. Johnson signed into law the Voting Rights Act).

WOMEN MENTORING WOMEN

In a cultural climate like this, it's important for women to keep our chins up, remain positive, and keep up with men both intellectually and sometimes physically. It's also important to find female mentors.

I connected with some of my earliest female mentors at the National Foundation of Funeral Service Women's Conference, an organization founded by my dad in the early 1980s, shortly after I came into the business in 1979. I imagine he thought, *Wouldn't it be nice for Lisa to have some female role models?* Or maybe he thought I needed all the help I could get! LOL! The latter is probably the most true, but little did he know that he would die only a few years later, leaving me with other women to help support and mentor me. Whatever his initial motivation, the conferences were a great gift to me by helping me meet incredible women leader role models.

I was also more than six feet tall and a bit insecure about my height. I soon got over this, though, as I walked the convention floor with Sandra Strong-Fitzgerald, from Strong Thorne Mortuary in Albuquerque, New Mexico. Sandra—more than six feet tall, blonde, and known as the "pink lady" in her community because she used to skydive in a hot-pink jumpsuit—was a class act in poise and professionalism. I wanted to be just like her. Sandra was accepted by men and served with men, and she taught me a great deal about how to live in a man's world. She also gave me encouragement, stayed in touch, and made sure I always felt welcome at every conference she and I attended together. She went on to become one of the first female presidents of a national association, the Order of the Golden Rule (OGR).

Another important mentor for me that I met at the same conference was a woman and licensed business owner from New Jersey, Anna Louise Bongiovi. Anna was very active in the National Funeral Directors Association (NFDA) and the past president of the New Jersey Funeral Directors Association. Anna was one of the instructors at the women in funeral service program. Now called the Funeral Service Foundation and serving as the charitable arm of NFDA, the Professional Women's Conference continues bringing women together once year and has close to 200 women and nonbinary individuals who attend each year.

I would attend NFDA meetings with Anna during my early years, and it seemed she knew everyone in funeral service as well as many of the main supplier groups. In her, I found a role model who had moxie and grit. Although she was only around five feet two in stature and barely came up to my shoulders, she still had a large presence when she entered a room. Confident and outspoken, with a terrific New Jersey Italian sense of humor, Anna taught me to advocate for myself and not be shy in front of men in leadership positions. In fact, she would just walk up to the men in NFDA board of directors, introduce herself, and challenge them on an issue she had concerns about in the profession or in the association. These lessons from her became invaluable to me over the years, because— believe it or not (my good friends may not)—I was shy in my early years and very insecure. I lived in the shadows of amazing, strong, and outspoken parents and grandparents, and our generation was raised to be seen and not heard as children. Therefore, as I became an adult, I was not sure how to behave in this new world as an owner when I became the peer of some of these powerful men in the world's largest association in our profession, NFDA. The lessons I learned from Anna were essential as I navigated living, surviving, and thriving in the man's deathcare world.

In 2022, the National Funeral Directors Association honored her at the Professional Women's Conference for her contribution to women in our profession with its first ever Legacy Award. I was honored to be with her that day as one of her mentees, now a friend, to see her life honored in such a special way.

I've had support during my career from many female and male mentors who helped me find my way forward. This support helped me establish myself as a business owner and also helped me grow my confidence as a person and a woman. Yet still, I didn't fully believe in my capability to be successful, and this self-doubt affected my decisions as an owner. In fact, my lack of self-doubt and self-confidence led me to make significant business decisions that eventually turned into serious problems.

Self-Reflection Questions

- What role do appearances play in your professional life? What does that mean for you on a daily, weekly, or monthly basis?

- Have you ever felt out of place as a person with a minority identity in a business context? How did that feeling impact the way you acted or your goals in that situation? How did you respond?

- Who is a mentor to you who shares this same identity? What have you learned from them? If you have not learned from them yet, what would you like to learn? How can you ask them for help with achieving your goals?

4

Overcoming Failures
and Challenges

The phrase "trust but verify" was gifted to me from an owner friend after I told them about a horrible mistake I had made that came close to costing me my company. In fact, the mistake was so disastrous that I was at risk of closing Baue and going to jail.

The phrase comes from a Russian proverb taught to then-President Ronald Reagan, who used it in his nuclear disarmament discussions with Russia. Sometimes as an owner, I felt like I was in disarmament talks with certain employees, with the unions, or with the regulators of our profession. And I haven't always moved through those talks perfectly—or through the actions that brought us into the talks in the first place.

As owners, we will make mistakes. We will sometimes fail. It is always a learning experience, many times painful, and many times costly. We also have to engage with the failures of others. As I evolved as a leader, when I was confronted with a failure by one of my team members, I came to look inward and ask myself, *What could I have done differently to support them or better train them? Where have I failed?*

Through my career, many of my failures were in not using my head enough: Not thinking about all the possibilities of what could go wrong. Not putting enough processes in place to provide safeguards for the company and its employees. Not communicating well or being available for the employees to come to if they had a concern. Not verifying with my team what was really going on. Not checking in with others who may have reported to a manager and not checking in on what he or she was doing or not doing. Not trusting myself enough and not verifying things when I trusted others. As I assessed the failures over the years, there seemed to be a lot of "nots." These "nots" were definitely wake-up calls for me that I needed to and did learn from.

FAILURE AS A LEARNING EXPERIENCE

When I bought the business in late 1989, later that year, I brought my then-husband and father of my children, Michael, into sharing ownership. He worked in the profession and had a keen financial mind and an MBA, and he had moved out into the corporate world for a few years very successfully. When he stepped into the business with me as co-owner, I relied on him to take care of most of the financial areas in which I didn't yet feel fully confident.

Working together, even though it had made sense to us both, eventually proved too hard on our marriage, and as the years went on, it became clear that, for a number of reasons, we needed to part ways. I did learn a great deal from him during our four years of ownership together, especially in the financial management areas of business. I've always been grateful for the training and gifts he gave me. When we ended our marriage and business relationship, I felt more confident in my financial abilities, yet his leaving still left a number of gaps I needed to fill.

One involved management. I had found that learning to manage others was not as easy as it looked, nor did it come naturally to me. I am a blend of an introvert and extrovert, and my tendency then was to lead with a dominant and direct communication style rather than being a patient, good listener, as this was not a skill I had learned yet. I also thought out loud and would sometimes say things critical of others without really knowing I had hurt their feelings. I would simply and straightforwardly say how I felt. I recall my dad telling me as I grew up that I needed to engage my brain before my mouth. Sometimes, as an owner and manager, I found I didn't. I would say things and regret them later—not a great trait when managing people.

When Michael and I co-owned the business, though, he was much better at being a caregiver to the staff. In his absence, I had to make my own way and make my own mistakes in this area. Some of these mistakes, in my own behavior and in my hiring practices, contributed to yearslong struggles with unions. They, too, became wake-up calls and deep learning experiences.

I first became aware of the unions when, as a young girl, I went to a Lutheran grade school directly across the street from our family's funeral home. I remember one day walking down the sidewalk and having to pass a couple of Baue staff members carrying signs. The men said hello politely as I walked by, but they seemed different from the other times I'd seen them. Now they seemed unfriendly and upset. I asked my dad what they were doing, and he shared that they wanted to be paid more money to do their jobs. When I asked why he and my grandfather didn't pay them more, he said the business couldn't afford it. Eventually, these men went away and never worked for my dad and grandpa again. And while I recall a few family conversations about these men over the years, seeing people with signs walking outside the funeral home in my childhood was something that never seemed to happen again.

As I became a funeral director, I realized the many reasons why unions didn't fit well in funeral homes. I was once sent to another funeral home to deliver our hearse so they could use it for a funeral. It would have been much simpler for me to just drive the hearse in the funeral myself instead of delivering it and sitting in their lobby until the funeral was over and I could take it back. I wasn't allowed to drive it in the funeral myself, though, as I wasn't in the drivers' union.

I recall a discussion with my dad on this, who shared that he didn't believe unions had a place in our profession, and especially with small firms. Unions, he said, would necessitate having to raise our prices to our client families. They would also restrict many of the services we could provide to families because we, as owners and managers, were not in the union. He went on to explain that unions were usually in larger companies with hundreds of employees who needed protection guarantees of their wages, benefits, and work schedules. Yet we were a small firm with fewer than twenty employees. He told me that as a small family-owned business, we could only afford so much in salaries and benefits, and a union contract could cause us to change how we did business and affect our customer service. I still didn't know much about the dynamics of becoming a unionized company, but once I became an owner, I received a hard and lasting lesson in using my heart and my head in paying closer attention to our culture and how our employees were being treated.

One day during my early ownership years, I received an urgent message from my general manager to call him back. He told me that he had left his wife and had moved out the day before, on Thanksgiving Day. He also went on to tell me he was in love with one of our staff members, his administrative assistant. After my initial wave of concern for his family, I thought of all the other repercussions. As an owner, your head begins to spin in these situations as you think of all the things at play and what can go wrong both for your company and for you professionally and legally. After we hung up, I called my attorney to make him aware of the situation and to learn whether there were any precautions he advised. He suggested I move the administrative assistant to another location and out from under this manager's supervision to hopefully negate any sexual harassment accusations in case the relationship did not last or ended poorly.

The following Monday, I arrived at my office to find a letter on my desk addressed to me from one of our area's unions. A petition was being filed by our funeral directors and embalmers, who desired to join the Teamsters Union. It would require a full vote of all dual-licensed staff along with our transfer staff in order to unionize. As I came to find out, over the years, not only did my dad have a union situation, but so had my grandfather. I guess it was my turn now.

I called my attorney and was referred to a specialty attorney in St. Louis that assisted businesses with their union negotiations until the vote took place, which we could schedule up to one year later. I learned more about what we could and could not do. Over the course of the year, we could not raise pay, give a promotion, or make any promises—that would be against the law and seen as persuasion, allowing the union to win the case. What we could do included formal and scheduled business meetings to educate the voting staff on what we as a company stood for and believed in regarding our treatment of employees, fair pay, and so on.

I could also ask the staff why they chose to join the union—and as I did, what I discovered was disheartening. It seems their manager had been treating them poorly. They shared that he did not come to help them when they were busy, and when they tried to talk to him about it or when they asked him about pay increases, he would shut down the conversation. He also told them that "the buck stopped at his desk." This was the same manager who had just left his wife. I, like many employers who care about their employees, just wanted to say goodbye to this guy right away and get his poor treatment of the staff out of my company. However, firing a supervisor during union negotiations was not allowed—it, too, would be seen as persuasion and trying to buy the vote of the employees.

I was upset this was happening in our company. What bothered me the most was that the staff did not feel they could come to me. It really broke my heart, and I felt that as the owner, I had let them down. When I was able to sit down and have this conversation with them, they said that their impression was I was too busy, my door was always closed, or I was out of the office or out of town. They shared that I did not seem to care for them or their concerns. They were also told not to come to me or it could cost them their jobs. They were being ruled by fear and feeling neglected by this manager.

How could he treat people this way? I thought. And the especially frustrating part was I still had to keep this person on for a year, until the vote was over. Mostly, I was disappointed in myself, though. My staff felt I did not care for them!

As the year went by, we conducted the meetings with an expert union business attorney supervising everything we could and could not say. I spent time with the manager I had to reluctantly keep on, and we worked on how he treated and spoke to the staff. I no longer allowed him to have meetings with them either one-on-one or as a group without me or another manager also present.

I soon began to realize that as good of a job as our company did serving and caring for our client families, we weren't serving our staff team in the ways they needed. The staff told me during that year of negotiations and meetings that they felt like the heart had left the company; people didn't feel like they mattered. This truly saddened me. I took personal responsibility for this culture problem, knowing I had failed and let the staff down, and I vowed to fix it when this union situation was over.

I really didn't know back then exactly what to do, but I did know that I had to follow the union and federal government guidelines in everything I did and said. I also needed to somehow find ways for the staff to know I cared deeply for them and wanted to improve our company culture for their benefit. So I did my best to become available and more approachable. I spent more time in the care center and on the front lines looking for ways to better support the team. I made it a point to get to know them more as individuals and ask their opinions on how we could better serve families and improve company culture. I did the things I thought I had been doing all along. I hadn't been doing them the ways my staff needed me to.

Trying to show them I truly cared for them combined with me being more present, getting the manager off their backs, and gaining the respect of the staff somehow led us to a positive outcome, and the union petition was voted down at the end of the year. The day after we won the vote, I walked into the manager's office and handed him his severance package and resignation letter to sign. He and the administrative assistant, then his fiancée, left the company around the same time.

TACKLING UNEXPECTED CHALLENGES

As much as I never wanted us to go through this again, the union issues did not totally go away. About four to five years down the road, we dealt with them again. We heard that the union had identified Baue as a place they wanted in their Teamsters' organization, so we believe they continued to try to influence individuals who were employed by us. When the issues began again, though, we were more prepared and found other and new ways to win the vote. Yet both times were expensive and costly to the company, running more than six figures each time in legal fees, and a major disruption to our business. And both times, I discovered we had supervisors who did not treat others well. Although we won both cases, they took their toll on our company culture.

These union difficulties went straight to my heart. After the second occurrence, which had come after I'd made some changes in being more present and approachable with my staff, I knew our leadership was still not leading as our team needed them to. I knew, too, that I was still not the kind of boss I wanted to be. First and foremost, I needed to work on myself and my leadership style even more, to be able to show my true heart to our people.

I had to be the first to learn how to improve, and at the same time, I also realized that I needed to find new leaders who had heart-touching management styles to help me. I began to realize that each and every person on our management team needed to use their heart in compassionate service for our staff and believe in a culture of employee care and engagement. As I started to make further changes in the management area, a new challenge arose—one that threatened everything in both my business and personal life—the one that almost put me in jail and closed the doors on my company!

Once my ex-husband Mike left the business and I lost the financial MBA mind overseeing our accounting office and company finances, I had sought to replace his position. Our company was growing rapidly along with the expanding population and death rate. It felt like it was all I could do to manage the daily operations, much less the financial side of the business. Also, it was a time in my life when I still was not especially confident in my own abilities as an owner to oversee the finances well, because I didn't have a business degree or financial background. So I decided to hire a headhunter to find a financial manager, someone who had the business acumen I thought I lacked and had lost when Mike left.

After reviewing dozens of resumes and candidates, I chose someone with a strong financial background, a degree in business, plus an MBA. Our new CFO could negotiate well, had a charming personality, and was a good guy raised in a conservative religious community in the region. He seemed open, honest, and forthright. His recommendations were stellar. He had managed several businesses in his previous positions and came highly recommended by others I knew and respected.

All went well in our work together for a few years, including through our union struggles, until the tragedy of 9/11 happened. In the aftermath of the attacks and the resulting stock market crash, the growth in our business investments along with our trust accounts declined. Yet at that time, I had believed our business was doing well. We had been growing in the years after I bought it, both in the time my ex-husband owned it with me and in the first years after he left, when I brought in our new CFO. Then, I received a phone call from our preplanning trust company. They were curious why our trust-fund deposits that came from preneed sales and those making payments to their plans had slowed down. When I asked for a report on deposits and reviewed it, I discovered that not only were the deposits sporadic, but there were very few made in the last year and hardly any in the last six months.

That seemed impossible to me, as we were on pace to sell millions in preplans that year. Deposits should have been being made monthly, at a minimum.

I went to my in-house accountant and inquired about the report and lack of deposits. He said, "I thought you knew."

Knew? I thought. *Knew what?*

Our accountant went on to share that the CFO, his boss, had him hold the checks and not deposit them until we had the cash flow to fund them. I still was not clear on why the checks were not being released to the trust company; according to the financial statements I received and the year-end financial review, we had had a good year financially and should be cash-flowing well.

Yet our accountant explained that was not the case. With the stock market in disarray, the interest earned on the trust funds we had invested in was flat, and I came to find out that, apparently, we relied on this to pay some of our bills. I was still unclear about what was occurring, so I went to visit my CFO. He explained that we had been in a tight situation since 9/11 with the stock market tanking. We had needed the interest earned from the trust funds to meet budgetary needs, he said, and without it these last two years, he had had to hold some of our deposit checks to the trust to use for operational expenses.

Now, I was not a CFO or an accountant, but I did know my regulatory laws and knew this was not just a small problem. It was *not* what we were supposed to do according to our preneed deposit statutes. The CFO directed me to the language in the law that said we "were to deposit 80 percent of the funds received" and noted the law was unclear as to *when* the funds had to be deposited. He had thought it was okay to use the income from the preneed payments to pay some bills while being able to release the checks he had written to the trust company as cash flow improved. I asked to see the checks he was holding, and he led me to a fireproof file drawer. He opened it, and as I looked at the checks, all signed by him and not dated, in several stacks which seemed more than a foot high, I felt the blood rush out of my head. What he had been doing was not "technically" in accordance with our trust statutes, and I knew we as a company could be in big trouble.

My next step was to call my business attorney. After consulting with him and adding up the checks, I discovered the deposits amounted to close to $3 million. We did not have this amount available in cash to correct this problem. My next call was to my banker. After looking over our finances and appraising our properties, he agreed to lend us the funds so we could deposit the checks as quickly as possible and make all our trust funds whole.

During the time we were working on the financing of the bank loan, I went to my CPA firm to discover how over the last two years, they did not know about the undeposited checks. I trusted that in their annual tax review, they reviewed all the companies thoroughly. In fact, their annual review reports stated in their "Notes to Finance" that 80 percent of the preplan funds were deposited. They shared that they had never been asked to audit the funds in the past. They were able to see funds received and checks written to the trust. Unfortunately, they didn't verify whether the trust company had received the funds, and I came to find out there were no management reports that tracked income to deposits. So I trusted my accounting review firm, and I trusted my CFO and my-house accountant to do what we had always done well, and I failed to verify that they were following all statutes.

This situation seemed like a potential disaster if it was not rectified, which I fully intended to do as quickly as possible for our company. What had happened was not right, and it had happened under my watch. I began once again to question myself and my judgment. Was I horrible at ownership? What did I miss, and why? Because I was not feeling confident in the financial oversight areas, I trusted others and their judgment without verifying.

I am a strict rule follower, a very black-and-white person, when it comes to the law. Moreover, honesty is one of my core values for both me personally and my business. I had a lot to grapple with. As a business owner, I needed to trust that others were acting in accordance with the statutes that they had been trained on and aligned with my core values. Had I trusted the wrong person? Was this a deliberately dishonest act that my CFO committed? I didn't think our CFO was a bad or dishonest person. I think he thought he was doing his best, juggling what he could to help us navigate difficult financial waters. Yet this poor decision could have the potential to ruin my family business and its future. And what about my in-house accountant? He was only doing what his boss told him to do, assuming that I knew this was happening, so he never questioned the right or wrong of it. I thought he, too, knew the law. However, he also shared the same comment that there was no definitive timeline that stated when the funds had to be deposited. In further investigation with my attorney, we discovered this was true. The statutes did not then say when the funds needed to be deposited; there was no timeline or number of days stated, and so my CFO and accountant were technically correct.

Regardless, as a standard best business practice, I always assumed that the preneed payment funds would be deposited into the trust within a few weeks of receiving them, and that is what we had always done until the year after the stock market crash. I beat myself up badly during this entire process of auditing the trust funds, borrowing the money, and making everything right. I was also determined to ensure that something like this could never happen again. I put new checks and balances in place to ensure that the payments and deposits matched up and the CPA firm audited them annually instead of simply performing a review. I knew the right thing to do, and I set about doing it immediately.

When an owner borrows money, we have to personally sign off on the debt and be able to afford to cash-flow the interest and principal payments. To be able to do this, I had to make some tough decisions to reduce expenses and improve cash flow during a time when our country was in an economic crisis. I proceeded to immediately cut back as much as I possibly could, starting with myself by giving myself a personal pay cut. I also began to pay closer attention to where we were spending money, spending countless hours going deeper into our company's bills. Before, the approvals of spending were all landing on the CFO's desk. That practice stopped. In the aftermath of this situation, I went into micromanagement mode. This isn't a great place to be as an owner of a sizeable growing business, but at that time, it was my responsibility to make things right. I was determined to ensure that nothing like this would ever happen to our company again.

The big wake-up call lesson I took away from all of this was that I needed to be more confident in my abilities and use my head more! I needed to keep a closer eye on the processes and procedures in our company and make sure everyone who handled money knew and followed our laws and would feel comfortable coming to me if they didn't understand something. Additionally, I learned that the owner always needs to know what is going on no matter how large a company becomes. It was important to trust (although it took me time to get back to this) but also to verify.

I took a big breath after this situation was all over and knew I had to make some new staff decisions. I parted ways with the CFO. A few months after this, my in-house accountant decided to announce his retirement. It was a great time to take a serious look at how to better operate my growing family business, especially in the area of financial management.

My owners study group was a huge support to me at this time, and they were able to remind me that we are all human and will make mistakes. They, too, had trusted others who had let them down. With them, I was in a safe place with people who had my back. They helped me find the answers I needed.

My next hire was a new accountant with a CPA, and as a team, we were able to resolve the financial questions and problems. I began to learn more and more about investing and managing trust funds during this time when our profitability was having challenges, and it was good learning for me as an owner. Through these challenges, I also learned more and more about the financial side of our business, helping me grow as a more financially astute owner. I began to have more confidence in myself and my decisions and felt the company was on the right track . . . until one day months later, I opened the mail.

It was from the attorney general's office Eastern Division in our region. It seemed they had somehow discovered the information about the delay in deposits on the trust funds and were going to be investigating us. Another letter was from our state board sharing that we had violated a number of statutes, and we were to report back to them in writing and then attend the next regulatory meeting in a month.

When you're an owner, these are not letters you want to receive. They are serious and could mean severe penalties and possibly criminal prosecution. Needless to say, this was a time in my business career when I was truly scared. I really could not believe this was happening. Would I be going to jail? What would happen to the company, the staff, and our community reputation? This could ruin our business. I had done everything I could to get the company back on track, from cutting my salary and cutting costs to tightening our belts so we could afford the loan the bank was preparing to use to complete the payments to the trust company. During the entire time, we were honoring all obligations to our preplanning, and we were serving our at-need customers well. Yet the charges in the letters could change everything.

We had no way of knowing who had reported us. And there

was not much we could do about it anyway except to simply move forward as best we could. My attorney and I began to prepare for the upcoming meetings and to capture as much data as we could to defend our position. We had the bank ready to deposit the funds to make our trust funds whole; however, they would not release them unless both my company and I were free from prosecution.

My friends in my study group continued to be very supportive and helped me keep my sanity through this time, but this was my burden to bear. I had trusted people to oversee the financial side of my business, yet I did not check on what they were doing, and the possible outcome had become terrifying to imagine. I hadn't ever had so much as a speeding ticket, and now I was facing the chance of prosecution and jail time. I was a single mom, and if this came to pass, who would be there for my children? This was the scariest thing I had ever gone through in my personal and business life. I relied on my legal counsel and my faith that God would see me through this, praying a great deal for support and guidance.

I was also determined to draw upon every last ounce of my grit and, using my head, continue to make it right—all while upholding one of my core values of honesty.

FACING FEAR

Walking into the eastern district attorney general's office was quite an experience. My attorney did most of the talking, and after this, I fielded a group of attorneys' questions. We felt the meeting went well, and after we left, I looked to my legal counsel for assurances, and he gave them. We did all the right things, we found and fixed our own problem, we had a solution in place, monies ready to go into the trust were borrowed and approved, and I had done all the right things to put the solutions in place as quickly as possible so this would never again occur in my company.

Our next meeting was with our state regulatory board, an appointment I had set up to comply with their request for a meeting. I took this opportunity to share with them our findings and make some recommendations for future state auditing oversight, which did not exist in Missouri at the time, as it did in other states. I was fairly certain they already knew about my situation because normally, the complaints that occur come through this board first before they go to the attorney generals' offices. What I didn't know was what actions they were going to take.

I knew what happened in my company was ultimately my responsibility. I hadn't been as in touch with the financial side of my business as I should have been, nor did I perhaps hire the right people or stay close enough, watching their processes and actions. Yet I also believed I had solutions for our regulating board to consider that would support funeral homes in the future and ensure that funds were deposited in a timely basis. I believed that our statutes needed to be revised and clarified and that an auditing process should be put in place for all funeral homes in our state every three years at a minimum.

As my attorney and I entered the large banquet room, I saw the familiar faces of funeral directors from across the state sitting around a large conference table. Most were my dad's contemporaries, and some had been on the board when he was serving as chairman. We were asked to sit and given the floor.

I spoke about my findings, my solutions, and having the monies to put back into the trust as long as I was not facing prosecution. I also shared that as a growing company, processes and procedures would indeed need to be updated and changed. I also shared my suggestions that the state board clarify some of the gray areas in our statutes and that they needed to take stronger oversight in this area by conducting random audits of funeral-home deposits. There was a look of surprise on most of their faces when I made this suggestion, along with a few comments about the affordability of this idea. I said that our licensing fees possibly would have to be increased but that the board had a responsibility to ensure the safety of public trust, and funeral homes would need to bear the cost of this. I saw a few heads nodding as I shared my thoughts, and a few took notes.

Perhaps, I thought, *I did a good thing today by coming to the board meeting, owning my mistake, and bringing some good solutions. Perhaps I even gained a little respect from some of the members.* It seemed so, because later down the road, the state took action, putting in regular inspections and charging funeral homes some minimal fees on every contract to pay for the audit inspections. When I heard later that year that my idea was being used to have the regulations changed, I felt a small sense of pride that I had followed my dad's suggestions.

As we left the board meeting that day, one of the members asked to speak to me. He was someone I had met before at meetings over the years. At first, I thought he was going to give me some encouragement or share his thoughts about my presentation and ideas. Yet what came out of his mouth that day is still a bit of a shock to me. "Lisa," he said, "I called you a few months ago to invite you to spend time with me at my vacation home, and I never heard back. I was wondering if you were interested in us getting to know each other better." *Is this for real?* I thought. *Is he really asking me out on a date? Now?* I felt disgust rise in my throat. This man, twice my age, was making advances as I was fighting to defend myself and my family business. I realized in that instant, he didn't see me as a professional; he saw me as a sexual object to have a fling with. The interaction turned my stomach.

It took all I had inside of me to not turn away in disgust. I took a big breath and remembered my dad's voice: "Lisa, engage brain before engaging mouth?"

I apologized for missing his call. Next, I gathered up everything I had left inside of me and replied with a polite smile. I knew it would not serve me then or in the future if I was rude to him. I shared the truth that I was in a committed relationship. I told him I was flattered, thanked him, and, with my best "onstage" smile, walked slowly away to join my attorney at the door and leave. I went immediately to the restroom to splash cold water on my face. I knew I was about to really lose it. I felt anger, disgust, and hopelessness. I suspected that with him on the board and my refusing his advances that day, my company's outcome might not be good. I had done my best to present the facts and give my recommendations, and then, at the end, I felt degraded by a professional man in funeral service.

We can learn a great deal from experiences such as these. I learned as an owner that there are circumstances sometimes beyond my control, yet I was still responsible for my company's and my employees' mistakes. I learned to better oversee and improve our processes and procedures. I learned to find the best financial managers that communicated well and were strict rule followers like me, who saw no gray area in honesty. I learned to find an accounting firm that kept a close eye on the deposits. I learned to look clearly at myself and my failures. I also learned to be courageous, speak my truths, and always present myself professionally. I learned that even in the face of inappropriate advances from men, I could keep my emotions in check, stand my ground, and maintain my own professionalism, when needed. These learnings were both valuable and difficult.

As we came out of the storms, I knew I needed to work on myself as a top priority and, when I was done, look at my company's hiring, training, and policies and procedures. I had done all I could to make the trust-fund situation right. Now, I knew it was time to really make massive changes in myself and our company culture.

We did not have a strong employee development program in the company, and we needed one. We were growing rapidly in the number of families we served, and it took different skill sets to manage this growth. We had some people in the wrong roles, we had managers managing people without having the people-skills training for it, and we had no well-planned and executed training and development plan. We were a medium-size growing family business back then with about forty-five employees (full- and part-time), but I knew that we were going to grow further.

I needed to learn to hire differently as an owner and then help others learn as well. I also wanted to help others develop themselves further to enhance their strengths and skills. But how?

Self-Reflection Questions

- Have you ever experienced a crisis in your life or business (e.g., financial or cultural)? How did it manifest? How was it addressed? What was the result? How did it make you feel?

- Have you ever experienced a large failure in your career? What was the end result? What did you learn from your experience?

- Who do you rely on for advice and support in times of failure? Can they rely on you?

5

The Courage to Change

As I grappled with how to make the changes I needed to, I reached out to friends, family, professional colleagues, and some of my mentors, asking, "What do I need to do differently? What needs changing?"

Soon after, my friend John Horan from my owners study group invited me to attend a meeting in his hometown of Denver, Colorado. He had gathered a group of owners and senior managers together to learn more about the topic of leadership. And it was here where I began my journey to truly reinvigorate my leadership style, grow myself to better use my heart in the business, and network with other leaders as we together studied best practices of businesses outside of our profession.

We met with Larry Beeson, the founder of an organization called the Leaders Network, which sadly no longer exists. We soon learned more about leadership from one of Larry's favorite authors and well-known speakers, John Maxwell, whose book *The 21 Irrefutable Laws of Leadership* soon become our new bible to learn more about being a better leader, both for ourselves and for our companies. Larry asked all the attendees whether we would like to gather again and continue our learning and learn best practices together. Nowhere in funeral service did such a program exist.

Our small group of owners soon grew into a larger group. We began to bring key managers and other owner friends to the training programs so we could all learn together how to grow ourselves and our staff as leaders and take better care of our staff members. I felt then that this new leadership learning group, over all other groups and associations I belonged to, was going to be one of the keys to our business growth going forward. And it was.

At one of our meetings, Larry invited an organization to present about a new training company they were starting, Graystone Associates (https://www.graystoneassociates.com). Still in existence today, this company became one of the best programs providing the tools we then needed to develop our staff, offering trainings on topics from first impressions and how to better communicate over the phone with shoppers and difficult customers to how to best greet people who entered our buildings. Graystone also had funeral arranger skills training and helped us with ways to psychologically assess our people to ensure that they were the right fit for their positions and grow themselves where they had challenges. These assessments, called the Caliper, were used before and after we hired people to ensure that we had them in the correct roles and were developing them in areas where they would succeed.

Using these tools allowed us to make better hiring decisions, make better promotion decisions, and help people develop their talents and skills. It also showed us areas where they needed more development, which helped us avoid setting people up for failure.

CULTIVATING HIRING SKILLS

During my time in the Leaders Network, I learned that leaders can be developed—and at all levels of an organization. However, if overinflated egos exist inside someone, they may say they can learn new skills, but in the long run, it's not so easy. This makes hiring decisions very important. One of my favorite books on hiring best practices and teamwork is *The Ideal Team Player* by Patrick Lencioni. I learned from this book that it's important to find people who are hungry, humble, and smart. We can teach someone to be hungry and develop their intelligence in various skill sets; however, it's difficult to teach humility. In fact, in many instances, it is not possible unless the individual first recognizes they are not humble and then truly desires to become so.

People who are humble, hungry, and smart are incredible assets. Instead of thinking of themselves first, they think of and consider the feelings of their fellow team members and the needs of the organization. People who are not humble, on the other hand, will think of themselves first and foremost, which is more disruptive to teams. They will not be good managers, supporters, and caregivers of a business. Often, they are insecure and lacking in their own self-confidence inside, even as on the outside, they appear to know it all.

As I was learning more about hiring the right people, developing them, and training them, I was also learning more about interviewing skills. We were not large enough yet to hire a human resources manager. Instead, I and a few other managers *were* the hiring team, and we hadn't been having as much success as I would have hoped for. We had to fill a few senior manager positions with people from the inside and the outside, and none of them seemed to last or felt like the right fit. I had to find ways to improve in this area.

Luckily, I was invited to attend a workshop for owners from one of our national casket companies, Batesville, that was using a new and highly effective hiring program called Topgrading, based on the book of the same name by Dr. Bradford D. Smart. I was very excited to attend this training. It was not easy to learn to understand and embrace the Topgrading theory, but after two days, we had taken in a variety of new and insightful information. The last day, we applied what we learned by interviewing candidates for the company. We took these interviews seriously and had to prepare for them by utilizing the Topgrading format and developing some questions we wanted to ask in advance. The entire process—including completing the interview guide, engaging in the three-and-a-half-hour long-form interview, and writing our final assessment—took approximately five hours. This may seem like a long time to spend on one first interview, and parts of it did feel tiring. We went over the same questions multiple times, asking about each job a candidate had held that was included on their resume, even back through high school and college.

Yet when we were done, we felt we truly knew very well who we had interviewed. We could sense what type of person they were from the inside out and whether they were humble or tended to instead brag about their successes. We could surmise if they truly cared for others and would be a good team player or if they would be more of a loner. It was amazing how well this Topgrading process worked. After studying and practicing the in-depth interviewing technique and reading Dr. Smart's book, I felt more confident in my hiring and people-promoting decisions. Until I sold the business, I continued to use and teach others to use both the short- and long-form interview guides I learned in the Topgrading training I received to hire staff at all levels. These techniques were proven successful and still to this day are used by managers that I trained, many of whom are still at Baue's.

LEARNING BY DOING

Another leadership game-changer I learned through my involvement with the Leaders Network was about the need to focus on instilling a mentoring and coaching program in our company, where training and development took place for everyone in the company. I now believe this should begin from the first day of hiring. It doesn't matter how large or small a company is; everyone who works there should be on a short- and long-term mentoring and development plan, regardless of their age or experience.

In fact, if you look at the research reported about Millennials and Gen Z and their needs for mentoring,[3] you will learn that establishing one in your workplace is a critical answer to our profession's retention problem. I really believe that for all employers in funeral service and deathcare, whether you are a funeral home, cemetery, cremation company, or supplier, it is essential that mentoring programs become part of your company's culture.

This next generation in our workforce is looking for more, and they need us—the owners, the managers, and their supervisors—to better understand their needs and the core areas where they desire more learning and support from their employer. Mentoring is important. It helps them feel happier and more confident in their current jobs, they have lower levels of anxiety, and they are more than likely to remain in their jobs longer if they are offered opportunities to learn and grow. Mentoring is more than just on-the-job "tagging" or show-and-tell—what I call training by "tribal knowledge." I've experienced this technique myself and know the ways it falls short! Establishing a strong mentoring program will help you retain and recruit more in the future.

---

3   Grace Winstanely, "Mentoring Statistics You Need to Know—2024," Mentorloop.com, February 2024, https://mentorloop.com/blog/mentoring-statistics/#elementor-toc__heading-anchor-8.

The training I received involved a little of both when I was first starting, but as I reflect back, it was not what I had needed most, nor did it develop me to become a future leader. On my first day working at Baue's, I was assigned to the front desk in the lobby. One of the secretaries showed me how to answer the phones, what form to use if we had a death call, and how to read a copy of a summary file so I could give out information on arrangements. The entire training lasted maybe thirty minutes at the most, and then I was left alone at the reception desk to answer the main phone lines for the entire company and greet people at the front door. That was my new role: receptionist. I had no job description, no training plan, and no path that I could see for my development. I spent my time dusting and cleaning the parlors, the bathrooms, the main lobby, and lower-level family lounge; putting funeral schedules on the announcement board; and changing light bulbs in the chandeliers and lamps.

There were times that were much more enjoyable: when we were busy with visitations and had hundreds of people in our buildings, or when clients were at the funeral home needing help with memorial donations or setting up rooms with flowers and keepsakes. But as we were a small company back in the early and mid-'80s, we could go for three or four days without a death call, and on most days, when we were slow, I was pretty bored. I finally reached out to my dad for suggestions on what else I should be or could be doing. He handed me a stack of trade journals and books on grief, loss, and funeral service management and said, "Lisa, the best use of your time right now, until you can study for and gain your funeral director's license, is to read. Read all you can on funeral service, and learn new ideas and best practices." So that's what I did: read and read some more.

A few months into my job, I was about to sit for a test that would allow me to gain my license as a funeral director, and then I was hoping that I could make funeral arrangements with families and conduct funerals. In Missouri at that time, we didn't have a yearlong apprenticeship for funeral directors. What was required was to read the state law book, take the test, and if you passed, you received a funeral director's license. I had wanted to go to mortuary school, but my dad said that the only good ones were all out of state and he needed me there. The business was starting to grow quickly, and he wanted me licensed as soon as possible.

I was nervous the day of the test. In school, I was not a great test taker. I think it was because I did not have much patience to sit still very long. I had read and practically memorized the law book a month before. And I was excited to cross this milestone. I remember the test well. It was fifty questions, all multiple choice. There was often more than one answer that made sense, and there was a series of questions at the end where I had to compute mathematical formulas and calculate trust refunds. This was back in the day when calculators were not allowed, and I had never had much confidence in my math skills. My confidence levels went down to an all-time low, but I was determined to make it through. I think I was one of the last ones to finish my test. I'd gone back through the test again to make certain I had my questions answered correctly. Yep, I was a bit of a perfectionist, too. As I left the testing site and drove back to St. Charles, I hoped and prayed I did well. I wanted my dad to be proud, and I felt I had a little something to prove to our licensed team at Baue's.

A week later, Dad called me into his office. When he shared the test results, I was shocked. Not only had I passed, but I'd received a 100 percent! I honestly don't recall ever getting a 100 percent during my high school or college years. My dad gave me a hug and said as soon as my certificate of license arrived, I could begin making arrangements. From this point, I assumed I would be getting some formalized training on how to make arrangements or start sitting in with the other directors on arrangements. But that never happened.

About a month later, I was eating lunch one day, and the phone rang. It was my manager asking me to come downstairs. He handed me a file and shared that I had a family to meet. You never forget your first family. To this day, I remember their name. As we walked down to the arrangement office, I remember being nervous, but after the introductions, I decided what I wanted to do next. I decided I wanted to get to know them and their mother, Rose, who had died. I also knew the form in my file had to be filled out at some point and merchandise needed to be selected. But that didn't seem important to me somehow at that moment. Getting to know them just felt like the natural and right thing to do.

Today, as we train funeral director arrangers, we call this the icebreaker time, and it is an essential—if not the most important—part of the arrangement conference. It is really impossible to help families if we do not take the time to get to know them and understand their relationship to the decedents as well as to each other. Some families are very open, some are very closed, and sometimes, the circumstances of the death, especially the tragic ones, can make it difficult to reach people and help them open up. To this day, I ask first and foremost about the decedents so I can help the survivors create a lasting memory and life-honoring event that both reflects the life of the individual who has died and meets the mourners' needs as well. This is not always easy, but it is necessary if we are to serve a family well and be able to personalize the service to honor a life in a special way.

On that day years ago serving my first family as funeral director, I did what made sense to me at the time and began to ask questions about the decedent's life, about what it was like growing up with her—their mother—and their dad. As the family began to tell me their stories, I wrote down as many as I could. We talked for close to an hour. They laughed and cried, and I did the same. They brought me into their family memories, and I felt honored to be there with them that day. Some may find it odd that a funeral director would laugh and cry with a family, but I believe it is normal and human. More often, I would wait to have a good cry until I was at home. On occasion, I have been teary eyed and sniffly with a family, especially when I am with ones I know well. Whenever tears come, to express these emotions is normal, and I encourage it with families and our funeral directors. Tears, I believe, need to flow naturally, and in fact, emotional tears can release toxins in our bodies.[4] Thus, giving people permission to cry is a gift we give them as funeral directors. (I also believe in allowing them to make the choice of whether or not to reach for a tissue; I have never handed one to families I served, although we had Kleenex boxes on tables throughout our funeral homes so that if they needed one, it was readily available.)

After that first hour with my first family, I knew I was in the right place, where I was supposed to be. I felt good about that first arrangement because I believe that the time I spent with them was valuable for them. I had been able to be present alongside the family during heart-touching moments in their journey as they said good-bye and buried their mother. To this day, when I see this family out in our community, they remember me and I them. They knew that I truly cared for them, and that's what really matters.

I also learned from this experience that just putting someone into arrangements without training was not really an ideal training and development program. As nervous as I was, there was so much I

4   Ashley Marcin, "9 Ways Crying May Benefit Your Health," Healthline.com, medically reviewed by Timothy J. Legg, updated April 14, 2017, https://www.healthline.com/health/benefits-of-crying.

did not know and needed to learn before I became a better arranger. Luckily, I had a deep desire to learn.

Time and time again, there has been so much to learn—and as a leader, I now know there is so much to teach. As a manager, it's essential to have the learning tools, training programs, role-playing exercises, and curriculum in place that will help you and your team advance in their skill sets. And whatever our role, it's essential to also have the courage to acknowledge where we need to improve and then embrace a willingness to learn and change.

Self-Reflection Questions

- Have you ever experienced or participated in a major overhaul of in-house processes at your business or in your work life? What did you learn?

- What skills did you learn on the fly when starting out in your career or are you learning now?

- Do you wish you had been taught those same skills in a more organized way? What could have been improved about your learning experience?

- In your role now, what business-related skills have you taught others? What do you learn from those interactions?

6

Showing My Heart

We all get messages that signal we need to grow in some way. Sometimes, these messages can be subtle little hints that show up during our business and personal lives. Sometimes, they are large and insistent—like when your employees file to unionize, a sexual harassment claim is filed against one of your managers, you discover staff are lying to you or are breaking laws, or your marriage or other relationship is on the rocks or even breaks up. All of these have happened to me. We sometimes learn in easier ways, and we sometimes do not. And sometimes, we have to be hit by the proverbial wake-up call that lands on your head, like a swing from a baseball bat.

Even though you can't miss a hit like this, you still have a chance to listen or ignore it. And I'm glad I can say that when life has delivered my strongest wake-up calls, I listened.

After our second union situation, I knew I needed to change and work on my leadership skills in order for our company to continue being successful. I knew I needed to change how I was as a leader for our company culture to turn around. And this led me to the phenomenal groups I talked about in the last chapter. Learning from them was pivotal in making changes in my leadership style and skill set. When that journey began, I set off on a path that had a powerful impact on both me and our company. Yet I didn't make all the changes I needed to overnight. I grew over time.

First, I learned how to better hire, manage, and get the right people in place so they could take care of our people well. And I tried to become more accessible and present to my team. This all mattered to not just me but more importantly to them and was the result of considerable effort and dedication to make changes. I knew, though, that still all the pieces hadn't fallen into place. I knew there was more learning and growth meant for me.

Next, as we continued to work on our staff training and development programs, we discovered we still had some serious culture problems. Feedback indicated that people were still not feeling as loved and cared for as I had hoped; it seemed maybe we had more changes to make as a company. I had spent so much time focused on training that I was not listening much to the front lines and the hearts of the people.

This is why one day I found myself in a crowded van with other owners, driving from the Denver airport to a place near Estes Park and the Continental Divide called Peaceful Valley. I was going there to seek the answers to becoming a better leader, to learn more from my leadership failures, to learn from others, to learn more about myself, and to hopefully change for the better.

Change from the inside out is not easy. It takes time, too—for me, time for self-reflection, time for journaling, time alone to really think about what is going on in my heart and my head. All this can be a challenge for a borderline introvert–extrovert with a little ADHD thrown in, but it was, as I was about to learn, essential to my ability to grow into a better person and a better leader. My company needed me to improve my leadership and communication style. My staff needed it; my children needed it. And most importantly, I needed it.

I hoped for inspiration at Peaceful Valley, but little did I know that my time there would lead to one of the biggest wake-up calls of my life as a woman, an owner and funeral service professional, a mother, and an all-around human.

TAKING STOCK OF YOUR (WHOLE) LIFE

We settled into our cozy mountain cabins, which were complete with a small living room and individual Jacuzzis. We came together as a group early that evening for dinner in the main lodge to meet with old friends and meet some new ones. We came into the retreat thinking we had one thing in common: We owned or managed funeral service companies. We discovered something else we shared, though: We were all relatively stressed out, or what today we might call burned out. Business and its demands were sucking our energy and our time away from our families, away from ourselves, and many if not most of us knew we needed to commit to making some changes. We were also all there to learn more about how to grow and improve ourselves as leaders.

This is what we expected of our time together. What we did not know was that it was also going to be a very emotionally draining time, full of self-disclosure and self-discovery. This was something I had never done—sharing my disappointments in myself with others I did not know well. We also spent a lot of time alone to journal and reflect personally on areas of our lives we wanted to change.

Our first day began by learning and sharing more about ourselves. We had to create a lifeline graph, on which the lines that went up were accomplishments and the lines that went down were sad, difficult, or failures in our lives, and then explain it to the group. As I presented mine, I began to see clearly that my life had a lot of highs and lows and, during some times, big zigzags. My early years had a steady line going up, from growing up in a great family, high school, and college graduations to working for my dad, getting married, and having my first child. Then, the lowest of the lows hit: my dad's death, the problems in my marriage, the problems in my business, the loss of more than one marriage, and all the failures I had had as a new owner, from the trust mess to the unions. It seemed like a downhill spiral, in fact; the zags down were bigger than the zig lines that went up.

It seemed like much of my adult life and career in the past was trending toward the bottom of the graph, except for a rise when I bought the business and when my children were born. The rest seemed to be about losses, not many successes. After I drew my lifeline, it was clear to me that my personal life was a mess and needed fixing in addition to my leadership performance. (*Hmmm*, I thought, *are they related?* Of course they were!)

Sharing this with others was hard. I am not good at self-disclosure with respect to feelings or things that happen in my personal life. I was raised to be a tough German woman who picked herself back up from failure and plowed through it to "get back on that Shetland pony another day." I had a heart, a kind and generous heart, but I just didn't let others see it very often. Why not? Back then, it was probably because I thought it was a sign of weakness. Baues didn't cry. Baues were tough.

But in that moment when I presented my lifeline, I began to cry, right there in front of the group. I did not feel that my life was a success, with the exception of having my amazing and talented son and daughter, who were my world. It was true I had some business success, too, building a beautiful new combination Funeral and

Memorial Center at my cemetery that was taking off in volume. Life should have been good back then. However, my personal life was a mess. I had to hire nannies and babysitters as a single mom and didn't feel like I had time to spend with my children. I wasn't exercising like I used to or finding time for myself. On top of it all, and even after all we'd been through and all I'd tried to improve things, my staff was still not feeling loved and cared for.

I felt like a failure. My lifeline seemed full of disasters, downturns, and bad decisions. I could not see all the good that had happened, as it seemed outweighed by the bad. I had a good cry that day in front of the group. Everyone was kind, caring, and compassionate. They gave me hope and an understanding that they were there for me.

In that moment, I realized I was not alone. Every leader in the room had losses, business mistakes, and personal crises. My story did seem to have a lot more than most, at least to me, but it was comforting for some reason to hear others' stories and realize they were not perfect either. They had made mistakes, had regrets, had disasters happen on their watch. I felt a huge weight come off my shoulders that day. I had people in that room who truly cared for me as a person and also understood much of what I was experiencing.

Most of us were perfectionists, and we were all hard on ourselves. It has always been my natural tendency to blame myself for my mistakes. Sometimes, I can beat myself up pretty well. Being at this retreat challenged me to look at things differently. Perhaps I needed to forgive myself, work more on my self-confidence, and focus on developing myself as a better leader so that I could better help others. It was time to let go of things I couldn't control and focus on what I could. For the first time in a long time, I wanted to spend time focused on my own self-development.

The rest of the retreat was spent learning the value of journaling, supporting each other through hard times, trust, teamwork, and authentic leadership in which individuals openly communicate their thoughts and hearts with all they work with. This last piece was entirely new to me, but I was learning how important it was. As part of our new learning, we did exercises as a group on how to better work as a team using both our hearts and our heads and improving our communication skills with each other. We learned to let go and to become more trusting of each other. Letting go of control is a hard thing for many owners and managers. It comes from a strong sense of feeling responsible for the outcome as well as feeling embarrassed if we fail. For perfectionists, this is not a comfortable place to be. We learned to forgive ourselves. We set our goals for the next five years for our own personal growth and success. We designed our bucket lists of fun things we wanted to accomplish. Our time there at Peaceful Valley was one of the best training and development wake-up calls I'd ever had in my life and career. I vowed to use what I learned there and pass it on to team Baue and others in the future.

We learned so much, and I will be forever grateful to Larry Beeson for starting an organization that truly helped us grow as individuals and most especially as leaders. I will also be forever grateful to those who attended the retreat that week. They were kind, caring, and giving of their hearts and their time. They taught me so much. We had times of bonding and friendship that will never be replaced, and many of those who were present there continue to be very close personal friends of mine even today. While I had close, supportive friendships with other owners in the past, there was something different about the time I spent at Peaceful Valley. We were incredibly vulnerable and authentic with each other. After that week, I no longer felt alone in my world as an owner in the same way. I had also learned a great deal about myself, about healing and forgiving, about trust and the importance of learning to become a better leader of myself and others—and not just a leader who made the right choices, not just a leader who made the right hiring decisions to help her people be well taken care of, but a leader who was willing and ready to show her heart. I came home refreshed and renewed and ready to make some serious changes in both my personal life and as the owner of Baue's.

THE TRUTH HURTS

After my time at Peaceful Valley, I wanted my staff to have the same opportunity to experience what I had, so I sent a couple of my managers to another Peaceful Valley retreat. To my surprise, some of them did not return with as much enthusiasm for changing themselves and their leadership styles as I had. As I was to learn later, it was their egos and insecurities that held them back. As I learned in the months after they returned, they were unwilling to personally recognize the changes they needed to make in order to grow. Failure, for them, was difficult to admit. Being honest with themselves, with me, and with those they managed was not comfortable for them—nor would it ever be. These are traits that would hold back the new culture I was trying to create at Baue's. It was sad. I had tried to help them become better leaders, and it was not going to work.

What I also came to discover is that some people, no matter how much leadership training you expose them to, if they do not have solid emotional intelligence, if they are not truly authentic and caring people who want to change their leadership styles in order to help others succeed, then they will eventually cause failures in your company that will lead to major consequences. They will not be able to lead successfully and help you create a culture of trust. After I discovered that these certain managers did not benefit from Peaceful

Valley and could not make the transition to becoming the type of leaders I felt our staff deserved and my company needed, I made the decision to bring Larry Beeson in to do a 360-degree evaluation of both me and my management team. I felt it was important for me and our managers to hear from our staff how *they* thought we were doing and how we could better improve our culture. I was certain this was going to be beneficial for all of us.

It was certainly for me. Yet certain managers did not care for their results, and they decided their staff had misjudged them. I began to listen to the results as indicators that I needed to make some changes in the team makeup. I think sometimes the truth hurts enough that some people don't want to face it and will do anything, in fact, not to accept it. But with this 360-degree evaluation, it was clear that certain managers were not well respected. It reinforced what I knew: The majority of staff at team Baue was not feeling well cared for, and there was a severe lack of trust within most of the organization. It was no wonder that we'd had the union challenges in the past. It was no wonder that I was not hearing the truth from the front lines. I knew I had to begin to make plans for changes; however, I believed it was important to work on myself first.

I was to rate myself and also have the rest of the company rate me, from my direct reports to the front lines. What I learned was a good jolt that all owners should experience. When I went in to receive the results of my 360, I found out that I was still not the best of leaders in our people's eyes. They felt I was not empathetic toward them and not a good listener. They still did not feel I really cared for them and that I cared more about our client families' satisfaction than I did for theirs. Even though this was hard to hear, it was just what I needed. Some people can handle a 360 evaluation, and some cannot. I felt I had let our people down, but I was grateful for the feedback. I was determined to fix myself and my leadership style. The staff at Baue's needed me to care for them as much as, if not more than, I cared for the families we served.

The managers who could not accept or acknowledge the results of their 360s could not remain with us much longer if they were unwilling to recognize the changes that were needed in order to become authentic leaders. At that time, I was unsure if I could work on changing me and the managers all at the same time. My goal was to become more outwardly heartfelt and approachable, and I was hoping that if I led by example, my managers would follow me and perhaps be willing to change as well.

I set out on a new path of learning. I had more one-on-ones, spending quality time with the staff, letting them know they were my first priority. I shared my goals of wanting to be a better listener for them. I wanted them to feel that I, as the owner, sincerely cared for them and that we, as a company, needed to do better to meet their needs.

After Larry left, I continued to have one-on-ones with every team member at Baue's—all sixty-plus of them, working full- and part-time. It was what Jim Collins in his business book *Good to Great* calls a BHAG: A Big Hairy Audacious Goal! I could not sustain these meetings realistically and long-term on a monthly basis and needed our management team to join me, but during that critical time in the culture change, they were valuable. I knew that I had to work harder and smarter to listen personally and more closely to the people on team Baue. I came to learn more than I ever had before. And I knew that this listening and personal time with the staff was the missing piece needed to set us on a path of changing the Baue culture for the better.

We established a core purpose statement for our company, and it was "To touch hearts as we honor life." At Baue, we devoted ourselves to holding and touching the hearts of the families we served, which is a beautiful thing. It's a necessary thing. But I realized that I wasn't holding and touching the heart of each person who worked for me, and I learned it was imperative for me to do so going forward.

The path we were on became a good one. I finally discovered the key to becoming a better leader. I found myself in a place of love, joy, and personal job satisfaction. Along with creating some BHAGs, we also began working on company goals together that were SMART: specific, measurable, achievable, relevant, and timely. Created by businessman George T. Doran in 1981, SMART goals were taught to me by Larry Beeson and became incredibly helpful. Each of our goals that year and going forward would have one that was focused on our culture improvement: how we cared for each other, for example, or how we would work better together as a team.

It was an interesting time. Change does not happen overnight. It took a few years for some of our managers to realize that they did not fit inside this evolving culture of focusing on our staff's needs as a first priority instead of those of our customers or managers. Those who could not adapt moved on. I chose new leaders to help me manage the company, to become our next leadership team. With a solid new leadership team in place who had earned respect and cared about the hearts of our people, our company began to prosper and grow like it never had before. It was amazing to observe.

Was it a hard thing for me to do? Sometimes yes and sometimes no. It did take time. It took becoming a continuous lifelong learner of leadership. It took doing more 360s. It took bringing in a couple of great consultants on leadership and emotional intelligence to help me develop my staff further. It took time, patience, and new learning, and most importantly, it took continuous listening and spending time on the front lines with team Baue.

The end result, though, was worth it. Our staff satisfaction and customer service improved, our profitability improved, and our teams all worked great together. For the first time in our company's history since my early solo ownership days, everyone was working well in harmony—the funeral directors, care team, preplanning team, grounds and maintenance staff, and administrative team. I found new managers for our finance area and our sales and services areas. Some came from within, and one was my son, who had a heart for the people he worked with and wanted to learn more about management and the business.

My management team was now full of people who had worked the front lines with them and were trusted. The others came from the outside but were experienced in the areas we needed, and more than anything, they used their hearts each and every day as they interacted with others. The majority were women, and most importantly, they all respected each other. We had an incredible management team of smart, talented, heartfelt people who truly cared for others over themselves and wanted the very best for the people at Baue's. We showed up for each other every day, and especially in tough times.

We were finally using, and showing, our whole hearts in our decision-making. We were not afraid to make mistakes and shared them openly with each other as learning tools, and all the stars seemed aligned for us to be even more successful than ever.

It felt like we were finally on the right track to success. The future seemed bright!

Self-Reflection Questions

- How are you hard on yourself? How does this tendency affect your work? What could you improve by changing your perspective?

- Do you agree that the truth hurts? Is it hard for you to be honest about difficult things? What consequences have you experienced as a result?

- Have you ever participated in a 360-degree evaluation—in any position—or received hard-to-hear feedback? What did you learn? What changes did you make as a result?

7

Living Our Purpose and Continuing to Grow

It took me decades of my career and life to learn how to be the most successful, savvy, courageous, heart-centered leader I could be. I'll admit that in the early days, I was working sixty-hour workweeks, and they were killers for my marriages along with my effectiveness as a mom and as a boss—the very roles that were most important to me. Yet I understand why I did it. I can give myself grace for that. I was passionate about my work, and I had a number of challenges to grow through. Some of these challenges affected my ability to trust the people I was working with, and it took me some time to regain that. As I learned to look at myself, change my own leadership style, hire the right people, and make shifts in our company that centered our heart for our own people, our culture changed. My trust grew alongside it.

I didn't begin to recognize how ineffective I was until I had my 360-degree evaluation in my midcareer. Then I saw, so clearly, how unwilling I had been to delegate, let go of control, and once again allow others in our organization to lead. I saw, so clearly, how important it was to develop and empower others, both men and women, at Baue's to take charge—how important it was to mentor them to be better leaders, then let go and trust them.

REFLECTING ON HARD-WON LESSONS

Our company ran so much better when I let go, when I trusted the right people. And when I found more of a gender balance—a woman as a CFO, a woman as a VP of sales, a woman as an HR director, and a woman heading our Care/Prep Center, all working alongside our incredible male leaders—we really became a harmonious team. We became a place where everyone was part of a bigger mission, purpose, and vision, where we each lived out the company values every day. All of my wake-up calls helped me, and us as a company, reach this place. All of my learning had brought me to my greatest success as a leader.

Leadership Takeaways

I would like to share some of my biggest learning moments:

1. It is not about you; it is about the greater good of the team, the company, the association, or the organization. People who lead and need titles are not humble leaders and are seeking titles for the wrong reasons. Humble leaders are the most successful leaders in all organizations.

2. Be the best version of yourself you can be. Being authentic and honest, staying true to the company's core values and yours—these are most essential to your leadership growth.

3. When others let you down, tell them so. Have a conversation with them, and speak your truths. Be a leader who stands up for themselves in a professional and humble way. Then, move on.

4. Lead with your heart, always. Even though sometimes it gets broken, don't close it off or give up. Leaders who use their hearts to care for others on their teams will always be respected and make a true difference in both their lives and the company's success.

Humility

I've also learned that to be successful in business today takes a great deal of humility. As a woman in the profession, I believe that leading with our hearts and showing true humility are an essential trait to have, to develop and ensure that it is embedded in all that we do as we strive to become great leaders. It is also the hardest to achieve as women. We struggle sometimes with self-confidence, insecurity, and imposter's syndrome, thinking we are not ever going to be good enough. This thinking can then cause us sometimes to lead with our egos as a way of protecting ourselves and our hearts from hurt.

In my life and career, my heart has been hurt more times than I can remember. And until I learned to use my heart in a way that showed others I truly cared for them, I was not a good leader, and I know I hurt others' hearts because of it. For that, I am truly sorry.

To all the women reading this book, I encourage you to not give up on yourselves, and do not stop using your heart in all you do. Do not stop working on being a better and humbler leader, no matter how much you experience rejection, failure, and broken hearts. You can change the world or our profession. I truly believe this. For the men reading my book, I know you, too, have great hearts and compassion for others. Let it show, stretch yourself to show your heart to your staff, and if you struggle with humility, get to work on it, because your people and this profession need you.

My definition of a **HUMBLE** leader is one who is

H = Heart-centered, using and showing their heart daily in interactions with others

U = Understanding, seeking to know always how others feel

M = Mindfully focused on the needs of others, not their own

B = Being kind and authentic, speaking truths in a caring and loving manner

L = Learning leadership continuously from others, from failures, and from successes

E = Empowering yourself and others to seek training and development

Focusing on these leadership tenets and a heart-centered purpose helped me lead and grow in the ways team Baue needed.

A PERSONAL LOSS

In 2008, I reached another level of learning and understanding of our profession when I went through a deeply personal experience: my mother going into hospice care and dying.

Coping with the death of a close family member is not easy when you are an active funeral director. When my dad died, it was unexpected and shocking. I was numb, frozen, and not able to function because his death was so sudden and I was so young. I was forty-two when my mom's lung cancer was discovered, when she was sixty-two. Mom, the consummate doctor and nurse's daughter, was going to beat this, she felt, and I thought so then, too. And she did go on to live ten more years with only a part of her lungs—one lobe, the one closest to her heart. This limited her at what I thought was a pretty young age, but she continued to travel, volunteer, and enjoy her time with family and friends like nothing had happened to her at all. It was through this show of strength as a resilient woman, an active volunteer, and one of the pillars of our community that I came to know how my mom lived for twenty years after my dad died.

Yet she did have a terminal illness, and it also seemed to me she might be in denial of the inevitable. I served so many families whose loved ones had lung cancer. I knew there was no cure; they just learned to live with it. Mom probably knew this, too, but never let on. I think she wanted to remain strong for us all, as she did years before when Dad died. In the ten years since he had died, she kept living her life, traveling the world, and, I want to believe, looking forward to the future. She dated a variety of men. Some we liked; some were just so-so. Mom was happy and having fun in life, which is what mattered most to my brothers and me.

Before her initial surgery, my brother Paul and I decided we needed to capture her funeral wishes. I will never forget the nurse's face when she came to check Mom's vitals before her lung surgery. She asked what we were doing, because as every good funeral-home family does, we had our funeral home's preplanning guide and a pen out to record her wishes. We shared that we were making her funeral prearrangements. The nurse was appalled and told us that our mom was going to be just fine and survive the surgery well; we were not to worry. I then told her what we do and how it's important to plan our funerals in advance, always. Also, it was the only time we could get Mom to talk about what she wanted. And after going through what we did with Dad dying so suddenly, my brother and I decided we were going to make sure we understood her wishes with some type of prearrangement. We were raised by a mom who was a planner and forward thinker in everything she did. She was our Scout leader and taught us to think and plan ahead in our lives. Plus, we had a separate company at Baue's that had been helping families preplan since the early 1960s. After the nurse left, we all had a good laugh at her response.

The first surgery went well, and Mom spent another ten years with us living a good life. When she got the news that her cancer was back in her lungs nine years later and she had maybe a year or less to live, her response was interesting. She said to the doctor, "Well, shit, I thought I could beat this." Then she said she didn't want to feel this, so "morph me up"—meaning give her morphine so she was not in pain. I had never before been with someone who was dying. It is hard to know what to say to them. Usually, I am never at a loss for words, but that day in the doctor's office, I was. I wanted to be strong for my mom, so I told her I loved her, I was there for her, and she should let me know what I could do. In her perfect tough doctor and nurse's daughter response, she said, "Lisa, I will be fine. Let's go home."

As the months went by, we watched Mom change. While I'd lived my life in the deathcare profession and was surrounded by death every day, it is very different when it's your own parent. As funeral directors, we are used to being in control and in charge. But facing the death of your own family member is a totally foreign place to be in. Having a lack of control was hard, and it was frustrating, because we couldn't fix the inevitable, and we knew that soon we'd be burying our own family member. Using my heart as a daughter and a funeral director to try to meet my mother's needs in her last year of life was something I needed to do. The hardest part was going in to work during the week, taking care of others whose family members had died, and then changing hats and going to be a caregiver and daughter on the weekends—all while taking care of my children, too. I was functioning in three different worlds, and it took a lot of grit, a lot of patience, and a lot of heart to make it through.

Mom decided to go on an experimental drug to help prolong her life so she could finish some things she wanted to do. Some of the time involved events with family and friends; others were to solidify some things in her bequests to charitable causes. The time we spent together was hard but good. As survivors, we always have regrets that we didn't spend more time with our loved ones, and I was determined in the case of my mom not to let that happen. Mom was a very independent and private person and didn't seem to want me around too much during her chemo treatment times. Yet we spent many more weekends together, going out when she was up to it, spending time with my children, attending social, charitable, and cultural events. She loved music and the arts and volunteered at our local arts center, which was set in a remodeled historic railroad car foundry. It was there that we celebrated her life after she died.

Doing the things she loved the most that last year was important to her, so in typical Jill Baue form, she planned it all out. High on her list was to go back to northern Wisconsin to visit a lake and lodge that had become her favorite vacation place, both in her years with my dad and when she was widowed. She wanted one last visit and to go fishing every day if we could. That August, six months before she died, we did just that.

In order to have these precious moments with my mom, there was a lot to balance and plan for me during that year. I knew she was dying, and I knew it was important to spend as much time with her as I could. I had to plan with my team at Baue to take over the operations of the business so that I could be there for Mom when she needed me. My brothers both lived out of state and came to visit when they could, but I was needed to be with her at home on weekends. Being a good scheduler, Mom had a helper for the house who could take care of her day-to-day needs, and I became the weekend helper during the months leading up to her death. In the last months, I reached out to a close friend, Annie, who had a home healthcare agency and had just started her hospice company. I knew she would help me figure out the care Mom would need.

This was my first experience using a hospice company, and it was then, as we put Mom on hospice, that I learned the true value hospice brings a family. I learned that putting a loved one on hospice meant yes, we were preparing for their death, but it also meant that there were benefits to pay for medications to keep them comfortable. It also meant we had tremendous support that was truly there for us as a family.

Having never seen someone in hospice care, I did not know what to expect. There were nurses and a caseworker assigned to us, who kept us informed every step of the way. It was not easy to watch our mother deteriorate from a vibrant strong woman into a dying person. She lost an enormous amount of weight as she stopped eating for the last month-and-a-half of her life. Her brain was changing as the cancer progressed and took over her body, and her personality became very different. She was crabby and angry a lot, and, of course, as family members, we were the nearest targets. Hospice helped me understand how important it was to not take the things she said personally. Morphine has horrible effects on people's personalities. It keeps them out of pain, but when they are awake, they are not always very pleasant people. It takes a great deal of patience to care for someone who is on hospice. I am not the most patient of people, but I learned to be better, for my mom's sake.

Her last two weeks were spent in a fog, in and out of consciousness. She sometimes knew who we were and sometimes did not. The end came one early morning on February 12, 2008, when Mom was seventy-three years old. The night caretaker woke us up, and my brothers and I were there with her, watching her take her last breath. It was more of a gurgle that came from her. Some call it a death rattle.

As we were all crying, I looked out her bedroom window and saw a female cardinal bird. As it was sitting on a branch, a male cardinal came and sat beside her for a moment, and they then flew off together. Cardinals have always had a special place in our family. First, we are from St. Louis, home of the baseball Cardinals and former football Cardinals. Second, my parents honeymooned and vacationed at a place called Cardinal Lodge in northern Wisconsin most of their married lives. Dad would have these little cardinal stickers he would give to everyone for many years. I still have some in my jewelry case and wear them to Cardinals games.

There are many theories as to the significance of cardinals, from the Christian Bible to philosophers and spiritual leaders. They are seen as a symbol of hope, restoration, and the afterlife, and some believe that seeing a cardinal is a sign that those who have died are with us in spirit. What I do know is that cardinals mate for life and are nonmigratory birds that remain in their immediate area all of their lives. They work together as parents to assure the health and security of their family unit. That, in a sense, describes my parents, how they lived their lives, and what they did for my brothers and me.

My faith tells me that my parents are together again and happy. I am not sure if I could be in the deathcare profession without this faith. For me personally, my belief in God and the afterlife brings me a sense of hope that the next part of our journey will be a great one, in which we are all together in God's kingdom. I know that some do not believe there is life after death, and of course that is their choice. However, to be with families coping with their loved one's death my entire career, I have a sense of comfort in knowing that there is more to a life here on this earth after we die.

Seeing these cardinals as my mom died brought us comfort.

It was a difficult time, and I was so grateful to the support hospice provided to help us move through mom's dying months. I learned how many gifts hospice care provides to families, and I will be eternally grateful.

GROWING TOGETHER

Many funeral homes working with hospice today have shared that it is affecting their businesses and that many hospice companies have become their competitors because they are telling families they do not need funeral homes. In some cases, this could be true, but we never found this a concern at Baue's. In fact, in the last ten years of my business, we embraced working with, learning from, and educating hospice professionals. We learned all we could from them about death and dying. We spent time helping them understand our business, too, providing them with continuing education and tours of our homes, our crematory, and our care center. We discovered that many working in hospice hadn't understood what we do as a funeral home company, nor did they understand the value of embalming, viewing, and ceremony and how it can especially help with the mourning process after the death occurs.

We began bringing in Dr. Alan Wolfelt, a leading death educator and grief counselor in North America as well as the founder and director of the Center for Loss and Transition in Fort Collins, Colorado. Each year, he would spend time with hospice workers, clergy, and our staff to teach us about mourning and the value of viewing and ceremony. These are essential learnings for all of us to understand in the deathcare profession.

Hospice professionals became our friends, not our adversaries. In fact, at Baue's, hospice became one of the top three referrers of our services. And the more we spent time with them, asking them questions, teaching them about us, and learning from them, the better we were able to serve a family who was facing a death. It was a good partnership and one I encourage all funeral homes to become active in, develop, and nurture, from hospice tours and education to doing lunch-and-learns with them and bringing in outside speakers, like we did with Dr. Wolfelt, for coeducation. At Baue's, we had what we called Baue Qs: Once a month, we would visit a local hospice and cook for them as our way of saying thank you for all they do to care for families. We would join them for lunch, put on an educational program, and have a Q and A with them. We also started a hospice-volunteer-of-the-month program in which we would honor a hospice worker who was nominated by their coworkers for compassionate care. At the end of the year, we would honor all the monthly winners and their teams at a luncheon, at which we gave out prizes and gifts to thank them for all they do.

I believe our hospice colleagues can be our number-one supporters, or they can send their families elsewhere. It serves us well to build relationships with hospice providers, for the benefit of our own businesses and also the needs of our client families. We should always look at ourselves as a cohesive team in serving those who are mourning the loss of a precious loved one. Good leaders always listen to their markets. Listening well can help you find the answers to what your company needs to do better, do more of, and do less of. We made a concentrated decision to do more with hospice as an integral part of our outreach plan, and it served us well.

So did continuing to build our in-house training and development program. We had been providing more and more trainings over the years as I grew in my leadership journey, until in 2011, we brought them all together to create Baue University. With the help of Marguerite Ham of Igniting Success and our human resources director, we built a program that provided comprehensive training for each employee for their first 180 days and first year, whether they were working the front desk, providing maintenance at the cemetery, or directing funerals. We had a variety of well-organized and thought-out training programs that helped them understand each part of the business: They would watch a grave be opened, go to the care center and see how we care for the decedents, see how cremation happens, see how we conduct a funeral. We provided grief training, because we felt it was important that all of our staff understand grief and mourning—because no matter where they worked in the company, they might come across grieving people who might be mad or upset and need to interact with them as part of their job. We also taught leadership and utilized *The 21 Irrefutable Laws of Leadership* by John Maxwell to provide essential learning concepts (along with other required reading).

Our focus at Baue U was to educate our staff, training and developing them to become leaders in their roles as well as in the organization. We also had classes for our managers to teach them how to improve as leaders and teach them how to be good coaches and mentors. Not only did this program help engage our staff and train them incredibly well, but it also helped them feel incredibly valued. They each knew that no matter what their role was, we cared enough for each of them to provide thorough, thoughtful training and development programs.

Once, we hired someone who quit within the first ninety days, and when they left, they were asked why in their exit interview. They responded that people at Baue's were too interested in them as a person, and they wanted more privacy and less engagement. When I learned this, it told me we'd really accomplished what we'd set out to do. It was a powerful testimony to our staff and how we were able to create a culture of sincerely caring for one another and sticking by each other.

Our first week of training was entirely focused on welcoming a team member and introducing them to our mission, purpose, and core values. We referred to these in staff meetings, talked about them consistently, and asked all Baue employees to carry a printed card with them at all times. On this card was our mission, our core purpose, our vision as a company, our values, and our service commitments.

Our Mission:
To touch the hearts of those we serve by providing the very best value in life-honoring experiences.

Our Purpose:
To touch hearts as we honor life.

Our Vision:
To grow our company to be the value leader in innovative and exemplary deathcare services.

Our Values:
Honesty, excellence, compassion, and respect.

I'm proud to say that we created a culture that lived and breathed this mission, this purpose, this vision, and these values every day.

Self-Reflection Questions

- Working in the deathcare profession, what has been your experience with hospice? What are you doing today to become partners with a key recommender like hospice?

- Who else might you consider competition, and how could you work together to strengthen both your businesses?

- What ongoing training resources are available to you? Does this apply to every position at your company? How could these resources be improved?

- What are your business's core purpose, mission, vision, and value statements? How do you work to fulfill those statements every day? If you have not developed them, what actions can you take to bring them into your company's culture?

8

Finding Work–Life Balance

One of the things most funeral directors or owners do not do very well is create good work–life balance goals for themselves. They also don't tend to encourage staff to do the same. Maybe it is because we are caregivers and we tend to give up most of our personal time caring for others. Yet it's important. At Baue's, we ultimately spent a great deal of time helping our staff find that work–life balance, and we taught about the value of it from the day they first came to work on our team. We also kept discussions going regularly in various staff meetings and brought in guest speakers on nutrition and wellness as part of the Baue University curriculum.

I first learned the value of work–life balance and brought it back to Baue's after my time at the Leaders Network retreat in Peaceful Valley, where I realized how very little I had of it in my life at the time. After day one of the retreat, I could see that having better work–life balance was essential to my survival as a funeral director, a mom, and a business owner. On that first day, Larry Beeson, as our leadership coach and trainer, led us through an exercise in which we were asked to write down our personal bucket-list items, keep them in front of us, and, from there, begin to set goals to make them realities.

As owners, our work can be all encompassing since it is never a nine-to-five job. It's all too easy for business obligations to become the majority of our lives. With this personal bucket list, Larry challenged us to think of things we wanted to do that could help balance ourselves and our lives outside of work. We were also encouraged to reflect on our lifelines and what had brought us joy when we were younger so we could incorporate some of these beloved activities back into our lives. For me, I loved to ride horses, be out in nature, swim, fish, and snorkel in lakes, rivers, and oceans.

When I did the exercise and created my bucket list, I knew that what relaxed me most was being around my four-legged equines as much as I possibly could. I knew that I needed to get back on a horse again very soon and perhaps someday have them in my family. When I was in junior high and high school, my horse Tally resided at a fairgrounds facility in my hometown. Every day after school, I would visit her, groom her, clean out her stall, and, weather permitting, ride her. The facility didn't clean the stalls, so it was a daily need and taught me a lot of responsibility. It also gave me so much joy and a way to get away from the stress of student life for a few hours after school and on the weekends.

After decades without any work–life balance, I knew I needed to bring back the joy that I felt years ago on my horse. And as it happened, a Leaders Network leadership trainer, Marguerite, had two horses at her home in Colorado. We quickly became friends; I was also the only woman in the group, so we naturally gravitated toward each other. She invited me to join her at her home to ride with her, and with my bucket list in mind, I accepted. Off I flew to Colorado, where she lived. This began a long friendship that still exists today. We started riding around her property and, over the years, began camping and trail riding with her neighbor and horse-trainer friend Terry. Now the three of us ride together each year and occasionally venture out on our horses into the wilderness for parts unknown—even in our mid-sixties. From both women, I learned a great deal about myself, my leadership, my team, and how to be a horse owner.

I also learned to fall back in love with horses again. When I'm on a horse, the whole world stops. I have to always be aware of my surroundings, but it's an incredibly relaxing time, with mountain views and babbling streams surrounding us in the peace and quiet of nature.

I feel the same way when my body is underwater, and so to continue to check off items on my bucket list, I learned to scuba dive. It's very quiet; once you get down under the water and under the waves, all you hear is your own breathing. Just like on a horse, when I'm underwater, I feel my whole body begin to relax and my mind go quiet. I finally found the peace that I sought both on a horse and while diving or snorkeling among the beautiful fish and underwater scenery.

IT'S OKAY TO BE A LITTLE SELFISH SOMETIMES

Taking personal time off like this is vitally important, especially when we are in a stressful profession like funeral service can be. Our profession naturally comprises a large number of compassionate caregivers, and we have a natural tendency to always put ourselves last. However, we can't survive, much less thrive, in this world of death all the time without taking time for ourselves—physically, mentally, and spiritually. One thing I learned to do was set up goals to take time weekly for good exercise, mindfulness reading, and journaling. It was not easy being "selfish" and taking this time off, but once I started making more time for myself and cultivating better work–life balance, it gave me more energy to manage my business, support my people, and help our community.

Any business owner will tell you that the people-management side of the business brings some of the greatest challenges and greatest gifts. It takes a lot of energy. And if you aren't balanced yourself and filling your own tank regularly, others won't receive what they really need from you. And employees need a lot from you! It's your job to help them feel valued, find ways to help them feel engaged, gain their feedback, and make sure you know what development and training they desire and need. Whatever level of leader you are, working in our profession requires taking care of others, and if you're not taking care of yourself, you won't be able to do this as well. One reason I wasn't a very good boss for a number of years was in part because I hadn't learned to find my balance between work and my personal life. I would pour all my energy into the business and then take care of my children's needs, putting myself last. There can be guilt in not being present in our funeral service work 100 percent of the time, but we have to step aside in a mindful manner and remember to take better care of ourselves.

In deathcare, which can be difficult and painful emotionally, we must work smarter (using our heads) to find ways to get away sometimes. Those are things we learned in our leadership training: finding that balance. At Baue's, along with coming to emphasize the importance of employees taking time off and having that work–life balance, we did our best to make the work environment as stressless as we could. From our fun in-the-workplace programs, contests, and events to our break–nap–relax rooms, we worked weekly to find ways to help our staff find more joy every day. It's essential—and even more now today, because the next generation is asking for better schedules, better benefits, better work environments, and employers who show that they truly care for their staff.

If you work for a company that needs to improve and provide more programs promoting work–life balance and fun in the workplace, I encourage you to speak up and advocate for it! Help the owners realize that just because our profession isn't a nine-to-five job and never will be, that doesn't mean we should all fully sacrifice our personal lives and mental and physical health to do this meaningful work. My bucket list reminded me of how much life there was to be lived outside of funeral service. And embracing work–life balance in my life, for myself and my employees, was a gift.

My relationship with Marguerite also grew over those years. We rode, laughed, and cried together. We got ourselves into some interesting dilemmas over the years, too. From chipmunks announcing something scary in the woods to getting bucked off our horses to climbing and descending boulders and terrains we probably should not have been on, we had the time of our lives. With Terry, we became a close trio that found times each summer to get away from our crazy work lives and find mindfulness and peace with each other and on the backs of our horses.

Our friendship and my connection to Colorado continued to grow. Then, one day, I was sadly called to use my professional skills to support Marguerite when her twenty-year-old son Matthew died suddenly one March. I returned to the state, this time not to ride but to be by her side as she mourned the loss of her beloved only son. I have never had a child die, but as a funeral director, I have walked side by side with families who have.

That cold March day, I took my friend's hand and led her down the aisle into a chapel in Colorado to honor her son's life. I passed out balloons, I held her as she cried, and I spent time at his casket before we closed it and he went to the crematory. I have done my best over the years to be there for her during the hard times as she has mourned his loss, and she has done the same for me during my life's difficult times.

I returned to Colorado that summer for another girls' ride. We called it the duct tape ride because when we parked the truck, a bale of hay went through the back window right before a rainstorm hit. We had glass everywhere, even in the hay. Fortunately, we had plenty of duct tape and used it, along with some cardboard, to shore up what was left of the window as a makeshift repair until the window could be fixed. In fact, I learned on this trip that good horsewomen always have duct tape handy in the trailer and truck and even on a long ride because accidents happen, your riding pants can rip, you can use it to repair a stirrup or part of the saddle or bridle, and other things can happen on a ride that are just unpredictable (duct tape is good for deep cuts and gashes, on both humans and horses, too). Thankfully for this trip, we only had to use it for the truck window. It was another learning experience the three of us went through together. And it led us to probably one of the most beautiful rides we have ever been on, riding up a beautiful mountain range and across rivers to sit at a lake, Duck Lake, next to the Continental Divide, for a picnic lunch with our guide, Wild Horse Harry. Even in the face of that year's tragedy, we found moments of beauty and peace.

It felt like Colorado had truly become a piece of my heart and my new home for time away and time to recharge; there, I could find the peace and quiet I was seeking. Little did I know, though, that what was to happen after the ride was to change the course of my life in ways I had never imagined.

CHECKING OFF THE BUCKET LIST

After the ride was over, I was invited to a concert at Red Rocks. Another bucket list item for me, Red Rocks was one of the most beautiful rock formations and concert venues in our country, set just northwest of Denver. Terry and her boyfriend had invited me to a concert the day after our big ride. Another friend of Marguerite's, a guy named Monte, would also join in on the concert. I truly did not want a date. I just wanted to enjoy the concert, with no pressure, especially when meeting a guy who lived in another state. *What were they thinking?* I thought. Hmm, they must have known something I didn't. That night, Monte and I kissed for the first time to a song by ABBA called "Take a Chance on Me," and we have been doing it ever since. Besides being a drummer in a couple of bands, Monte was a school district librarian, the IT teacher guy, and a football and track coach. He also had a motorcycle. Our first real date took place on the back of his Harley Dyna Glide as we rode down to Colorado Springs and halfway up Pikes Peak.

Sometimes, when you begin a bucket list, you go through exercises that take you back to your childhood. My first boyfriend was a motorcycle and motocross rider, and we had spent countless hours on the back of his bike, much to my parents' chagrin. There is a sense of freedom being on a bike with the wind in your face on an open winding road, which I loved years ago and loved again as I rode up with Monte to Pikes Peak. When we got there, the views were incredible. We ended our ride in the small town where Monte grew up at the base of Pikes Peak, Green Mountain Falls. I was already in love, both with Monte and the little mountain town with its precious gazebo, small lake, and peacefulness.

After dating long distance for a year, Monte decided to move to Missouri with me after he retired from teaching. As we were packing up his house for sale, storing his furniture, and moving him, something just did not feel right. I realized that we belonged together, and we belonged in *Colorado*. Something in the back of my head and inside my heart had continued to draw me to the mountains, year after year. It continued to make me feel like I was where I was meant to be. Do we always listen to these messages in our hearts and heads? Not always, yet this one was so strong, and eventually, I could no longer ignore it. I knew I needed to find my way to Colorado on a more permanent basis.

This is impossible, my logic told me. *I have a funeral business to run; I can't leave it long term—or if so, I need to retire and sell it.* Monte and I began to dream together about the future. I promised him I would retire in five years, and we would buy a small ranch in Colorado, close to his family, where he could ride his motorcycles and I could ride my horses. I knew it would take me that long to transition the business to my son, John, and the leadership team for oversight and future purchase. John had completed his MBA, was licensed, and seemed to be interested in ownership, so all my plans would fall neatly into place—or so I thought at the time.

As we vocalized our plans in front of our realtor friend, she was taking mental notes. A month after Monte moved to Missouri, he headed back to Colorado for his birthday and to finalize the sale of his home. The realtor called. She had a ranch come up for sale out of foreclosure that day, and if we liked it, we had twenty-four hours to put a contract on it. Normally, I am not an impulsive person, and neither is Monte. Yet there was something about this ranch. After touring the property with his son, they fell in love with it and quickly sent me more than fifty images of the ranch. We only had that night to submit a contract. We decided to go for it.

It was my dream to live in Colorado, to ride horses. It was time to take a risk and make it happen. We ended up being chosen as the new owners of the ranch within thirty days. And I could check another item off my bucket list!

Life felt amazing. Yet I still owned my home and business back in Missouri. What were we to do now? It was time to be thinking about my future life and business transition as a new wife and a current business owner. I also needed to think about what I wanted Monte's and my future life to look like in Colorado.

Self-Reflection Questions

- Does the culture at your business support a healthy work–life balance? What processes, amenities, or accommodations are in place to maintain balance? Or if it does not support this balance, what action can you take to help improve the environment?

- Is taking care of yourself a priority, or do you consistently put the needs of others (and your work) ahead of your own needs? What consequences have you experienced? What self-care goals do you have for this year?

- What is on your bucket list? How can you make plans today that will help you achieve those goals?

9

From Owner to Coach

W hen I was suddenly asked to serve in an owner's role when my dad unexpectedly died, I did not feel prepared. So I was determined to thoroughly prepare my children should they ever desire to work in the family business. One of my requirements for either of my children to become an owner someday, in addition to their working in the business a minimum of five years, was that they needed to complete a college degree and obtain their MBA or something comparable before they were forty to help them understand owning, running, and managing a successful business.

Being a successful business owner is not easy. Whether you are a mortuary science graduate or have a business degree, getting your master's in a business-related field will help you gain the additional knowledge you need and will take you to a higher level of knowledge in finance, investing, strategic planning, and marketing, all of which will help you grow and develop a successful business in today's increasingly difficult economic and regulatory environment. During my career as an owner, I was so busy being a mom, a funeral director, and an owner in a rapidly growing community and business, I felt I didn't have the time to take on much else and go back to school for my MBA. This is one of my biggest regrets as I look back on those early years. Another is not having simply taken some business classes or gotten a business major or minor during my college years.

It's so valuable to get as much education as early as possible, before life, career, and family obligations get in the way. I believe that any aspiring business owner in our profession today should have a minimum of a degree in business, accounting, finance, marketing, or similar majors, and I suggest a minor in one of the others. If you do not choose this path of higher education or do not have the time or resources, it's okay. But understand that if you move into ownership, you will need to hire consultants and those with this knowledge to help you navigate the complexities of the business and legal landscape.

I knew this type of advanced business education would be invaluable for my children if they wanted to own and operate the business someday—an outcome I'd always hoped for. Yet despite their additional education, this didn't turn out to be the right path for either of them.

LETTING GO OF A DREAM

As parents, we want our children to be happy in their lives and find fulfillment in their work and all they decide to do. They do not always want to follow our footsteps, and that needs to be okay, too.

My daughter Erin had financial and marketing classes with her hospitality and management degree, and she had a great deal of event planning, culinary, and systems training. She also has creative and artistic abilities and is a social media wiz. However, she decided to pursue a different career direction. She had worked for Baue's during high school and college and loved the event side of our business, working under our event planner to put on community events and life-honoring events that some call celebrations of life. She enjoyed such events yet found funerals too sad; therefore, she did not want to come into the family business after graduation. I supported her in following the path that called to her, and she is now a senior event planner for a large direct marketing company in Las Vegas, which gives her great joy.

My son, John, who is eight years older than Erin, initially decided to come into the family business after graduating with a degree in sports management. He began his career after college by growing his skills in the management program with Enterprise, headquartered in St. Louis. There, he learned people management, dealt with various customers, and eventually had his own location to manage. He came to me after a few years, realizing he was not passionate about the rental-car business and wanted to look for something different. After exploring options with me, he began his funeral director apprenticeship with Baue's. He excelled in people relations, sales, and building community relationships. John became an amazing funeral director and used his people-management skills to bring teamwork and caring for our staff to the forefront of all we did.

During his career with Baue's, John decided to go back to school for his MBA at our local university and graduated with almost straight *A*s. I was very proud of him. He was a young man who'd hated math when he was younger (like his mom) and who did not have initial confidence in himself yet eventually excelled in graduate school. He learned finance and accounting principles that served him at Baue's, helped us be a better company, and will serve him the rest of his career. John eventually became vice president of our firm and used his MBA knowledge to help us a great deal during the years of his employment.

My son and I had begun discussions about transitioning the

business to him when I was in my mid-fifties and he was around thirty, the same age as I was when my dad died and I began to learn what it was like to be a business owner. As we began talking about his future ownership and he was offered the opportunity to buy some stock, he seemed excited. It caused him to better understand how businesses operate and how to manage debt. He took on more and more responsibility and was doing well in his more than eight-year career with us.

Then, things began to change. I saw death and grief wear on my son as he got married and began to raise a family. His desire to spend more time with his children and to support his wife, Emily, became an increasing priority. I believe that was the right thing for him to do, yet there began to be more and more challenges for him in finding the balance between the busy work and home lives he led. And the more he served families, especially the ones he knew well, the sadder he seemed to become. I am not sure whether he or I recognized where the unhappiness was coming from back then, but we both spent time talking about his feelings as we sought to understand them.

Eventually, I convinced him to seek counseling while he was questioning whether the funeral business was where he belonged. He came to me one day and shared that he wanted to try a different career. He was unsure what that was; he just knew it wasn't in funeral service. After a little more than nine years in the business, becoming licensed, getting his MBA, and learning all the areas he could of our business, he wanted to leave to find a new career path. As we sat down on the day he announced he did not want to continue and buy the business in the future, he said to me, "Mom, I just don't want the same life like you have had."

As I reflect back on this discussion and realization, I remember all the times that I missed some of his sporting activities or wasn't able to be there after school for him, and the many nights and weekends he had to have a sitter because I was working. Maybe he saw too many times like this, when Mom was not home and was instead at the funeral home. Being a business owner takes sacrifice beyond weekdays in the office. Work comes home at night, too. My children also saw the many stresses the business sometimes put on me. As a single mom, I sometimes found balancing all the needs of my children and my business difficult. And on top of this, I was with families at times who needed me and had tragic losses that my children knew about.

There were times when death affected me; there is no way to avoid it, because certain types of deaths can be horribly sad. I had personal losses and family and friends who died, and there were times when I had to pause, walk out of church, and put myself back together before going back in to finish a service. Maybe I thought too much of these losses, and they came home and affected my children, too! I thought I was pretty tough and could handle anything, but as I reflect back, perhaps my children saw some of my sadness too many times, and that's part of why they didn't want to own or be involved in this type of business.

I was sad and puzzled by his decision for a while and had to make peace with the idea of our family business not transitioning to one of my two children into the fourth generation. Yet I knew it was such a difficult decision for John to make to not remain at Baue's long term. He needed my support and love during this time as we transitioned the business in another direction. After he shared this desire to do something different, I recalled the letter in which my dad shared his feelings about how hard the business was, and also the conversation I had with my mom as to how it hurt my dad's heart. *Perhaps*, I thought, *my son is more like his grandfather than I knew.* As his mother, I needed to understand and accept his decision.

Recalling Dad's letter also brought me back to reality in reflecting how this business wasn't for everyone. For some, it hurt their heart so much, it affected their health, their mental well-being, and their ability to be fulfilled in their life's work. To be in this profession, you must have a great deal of resilience (grit), because you are serving people who are mostly always sad and mourning the loss of a precious loved one. It takes a lot of inner strength and a pretty thick skin to do this job day in, day out for years and years. Being around the dead, the dying, and the mourning is not for everyone.

I found that to be the type of person who thrives long term in our profession, you also have to have the ability to see the end results of the most gruesome of deaths and be able to not take it on fully. Yes, it will affect you at times; you will go home, hug your spouse or your children or your pet, and have a good cry. As funeral directors, we are human. We love, and we mourn as well. Yet you have to be able to deeply sympathize without taking on another's feelings or putting yourself in their shoes. If you can't do that, I advise you to reconsider whether this is the profession for you long term, especially if you wish to become an owner or manager.

My son, I discovered, is built differently from me, and that's okay. Not all of our children are like us, and hopefully most are better, different, and their own people, finding their own path in life. For John, he took a few years off, became a stay-at-home dad to his now-almost-four-year-old. It meant the world to him to give his children more of his time in their early and formative years, and I am so very proud of him for discovering this about himself. He is now back out working part-time in the business world and taking joy in the balance he found between fatherhood and work.

My dad was built differently from me, too. I think perhaps I am built inside more like my gritty grandfather, Pop Baue, and maybe my mom, a tough doctor and nurse's daughter. We are all built differently and need to honor that in the ways that feel right to us and bring us fulfillment. So as a business owner, I had to realize that selling outside of our family was an alright thing to do. And as a parent, I had to be okay with my children's decision to not have a career or life like mine. It was time to move on and plan together for the future.

Transitions like this take time. They take many months of soul searching, and they also take using your head and your heart plus your grit to get through them.

John and I spent more and more time discussing various options for him in the future while the decision was made to sell the business. We spent time thinking and planning together, and eventually, after meeting with business friends and consultants, we devised a transition plan for us and our family business. We both came to a place of peace with our decision, as hard as it was. I have many professional colleagues who did not understand my decision; some thought it was horrible and made statements that I "sold out to the corporates." There were many who have criticized my decision publicly as well. Some thought I should have continued to work, own the business for a longer time, and found ways to help it continue to be family or independently owned. Yet I know I did the right thing for our family and our company.

I was proud that our family business had grown tremendously in the years I owned it. And it was due to the efforts I, along with my son and team Baue, put into it. At the end of my ownership, we were serving more than 2,500 families a year with all of our business entities, and the options to remain independent were very slim because very few companies or individuals could afford its then-current value. As an owner who had worked for more than thirty-eight years in the profession, I was proud we had created one of the best companies in the Midwest in our profession. I will never apologize for, nor do my son and I regret, selling our company at a fair price to the Park Lawn Corporation in 2019. The business had simply grown too large for us to consider a sale to the staff or to an independent entity, as much as we really would have liked to have done so if possible. The financing and borrowing costs would be so large that they would not allow a staff member or independent buyer to grow the business further, which was what we wanted for Baue's. Park Lawn, by contrast, has been able to continue to invest back into the business and the community of St. Charles County, and for that, we are grateful and pleased.

The sale benefited the families we served, ensured that our staff had a great company to work for, and gave many of our management team members opportunities for advancement into positions in which they are still thriving today. The sale also helped me personally take care of my family. I knew I deserved to be rewarded for all my efforts as an owner who had grown her business as I had. During my tenure, I took many risks, had many challenges, and overcame them to grow a business into a successful market leader.

In the beginning of my ownership, my mom gifted me one share of stock to help me buy the business, and I had a note payable back to her to pay her back and buy out the rest of the stock over time. I discovered after she died that in her will, she reduced my share of her estate by the amount of that share of the stock she gifted and that she gave my brothers cash at the time of her death. I went into millions of dollars of personal debt to afford buying our family business. I took on more debt years later to buy out my ex-husband, then to buy some of our buildings that were in other family members' hands, and then I purchased a troubled cemetery and brought it into a profitable venture. I bought and sold and built funeral homes and had a lot of fun along the way, too. (Debt is a reality of ownership, by the way, and if you are afraid of it, then reconsider becoming a business owner.) During my career as an owner, I worked hard and long hours for years to ensure that the business cash flowed and grew while I also paid back the debts over a long period of time. At the end of this ownership journey, I was ultimately okay with the decision to sell it in a rewarding way and did so with no regrets. My son, John, made the right decision for him, too, as he owned some stock and was able to create a nest egg for his young and growing family. Living a life that fulfills you both personally and professionally is extremely important.

I have watched so many of my contemporaries and their family members wait too long to transition their businesses, with many seeming like they will never retire. I have seen owners hang on way too long, even dying while working full-time. I do not understand these decisions to not let go, to not retire, to not enjoy life in the later years. I knew it was not for me! I wanted to do other things in life in my sixties and seventies while I was still semi-young and healthy. I wanted to volunteer more, give back to the profession, travel more with my husband, and spend much more time in Colorado with my horses and in Missouri and Colorado with our growing number of grandchildren.

The day we finalized the sale and I signed the last document, I was sad in so many ways but also happy. In our family, we call it "sappy." I was happy to move on to the next stage of life. I was happy I had, with my son's blessing and help, shopped around for the right buyer and sold for a fair price. I was happy to be able to use that money to give back to my family, my community, and my profession. I was able to start a family charitable fund, provide scholarships and gifts to charities to better serve our community and profession, and make a difference in others' lives. I was ready to enter a new chapter in my life.

EMBRACING THE FUTURE

Some have asked me how and why I became a funeral coach and mentor after I retired. At a convention the fall after the sale of the business in 2019, I ran into my friend Dr. Alan Wolfelt at a national convention. He asked me what I was going to do next because he knew complete retirement was not in my DNA. I shared that I had a desire to help the younger generation become successful and learn to not make the same mistakes I did. I wanted to help them grow and thrive as future leaders and possibly owners someday. And through my interactions with them during the previous few years, I had discovered many were struggling, and most of them were women. When I described what I was thinking of doing, he looked at me, smiled, and shared, "You want to be a funeral coach." We had a great laugh at that one because it was a clever industry play on words: My dad and his generation called hearses funeral coaches. A new business was born (and thank you, Alan, for helping come up with a great business name!).

What he shared next, though, was an even more important gift. He said, "Lisa, I really recommend that you take a year off first and do nothing but just *be*." Alan knew me fairly well and knew that doing nothing for a year would be a very hard thing for me to do. But being a good student of Dr. Alan Wolfelt, I tried to do just that. I knew it was a gift I needed to give myself then: Slow down, do nothing for a while, sit with the selling of my business and any feelings around it I had, and think deeply about my future as a retired owner and a funeral director, who was now a wife, a grandmother, and just Lisa.

I am sure that Alan, in wanting me to think more deeply about my future life and what I wanted it to look like, felt it would ground me, to ensure that whatever vision I came up with would be the right one for me personally, based on who I was at the time and how I saw my future.

Following his advice was a hard thing to do, especially the slowing-down part, yet as a good student, I did as he instructed. I read a few books on retirement along with a few fiction books, traveled a bit with my husband, attended a few funeral conferences, and stayed busy with the holidays through the new year.

When that new year, 2020, began, I knew I still wanted to start my consulting and coaching company to help the next generation of leaders and especially women. I was ready to move into a career path I was qualified for and one that gave me a great deal of joy. But I did not know that my plan to become a business coach and mentor would come to a screeching halt as the worldwide COVID-19 pandemic unfolded.

Isolation was a difficult thing for everyone, but it was also a time of self-reflection for many. My son was still at Baue's as a funeral director and manager for a time, and he didn't want me coming to work in person for safety reasons. So I helped with some arrangements on Zoom instead, made calls to families I knew, and did my best to offer them comfort. It was a bit frustrating to not be able to help more—and also so very sad to see how the pandemic affected families, since they couldn't be with loved ones when they died and didn't have time to mourn together in person.

Team Baue became very stressed and burned out with the high volume of deaths they experienced. And I knew that to get through this, funeral service professionals were going to need a great deal of emotional support in the future. My son, after the pandemic, made it about a year before he was totally spent and burned out. Other Baue staff members experienced this, too, as well as hundreds and possibly thousands of employees, managers, and owners across the country. We don't know at what rate funeral, cremation, and cemetery service companies had staff quit the profession completely or move to other employment in the profession following the pandemic, because the deathcare profession did not track this attrition rate. Yet if you look at the Gallup research done on the Great Resignation, you will learn that the overall numbers seem quite large in the United States. In a 2021 article, Gallup reported that businesses over the five years following the pandemic are still "facing a staggeringly high quit rate—3.6 million Americans resigned in May alone—and a record-high number of unfilled positions."[5] I believe the Gallup statistics more than likely represented our profession, too; however, we have no research that tells us this is the case. And I feel certain, after speaking to owners and managers around the profession in the few years past the pandemic, that we were going through one of the largest changes in our history since cremation gained popularity, one that would affect us for many years to come and, I believe, still is.

The pandemic, and the months that followed as we came out of it, caused me to reflect on how my new coaching and consulting company was going to be needed even more. We knew that firms would be having staffing challenges, and we knew the death rate would be going down for a few years or more, because a number of people who would have died during the next few years had unfortunately died sooner than expected, meaning funeral service and related companies would have less revenue in those years to come. How much less and for what period of time were still unknown, but many experts predicted that a minimum of a few to five years would be the most challenging.

---

5   Vipula Gandhi and Jennifer Robison, "The 'Great Resignation' Is Really the 'Great Discontent,'" Gallup Workplace (blog), July 22, 2021, https://www.gallup.com/workplace/351545/great-resignation-really-great-discontent.aspx.

Some older owners would probably want to retire, like I did. Some would want to stay and would be stuck in a situation with increasing staff burnout and resignations and no one to sell their businesses to. On top of this, you had an interesting dichotomy: There were increasing enrollment rates at mortuary schools, containing higher proportions of young people—the majority of whom were women. Their graduation rates were beginning to grow as well.[6] Many of us believe that those who were touched by death during the pandemic decided to come into funeral service because of it, along with their strong desire to be in a caregiving profession to help people. Yet with increasing staff numbers and a decreasing death rate, there was a concern within the profession that there might not be as many jobs for them. As I was growing my coaching company, I wondered, Who would be out there for the profession who could help? Who would help the employers navigate these never-before-seen changes after the pandemic, with shrinking margins and customers? And who would help those new to our profession—and especially women, who constituted 70% of those graduating in 2021 (and today constitute 75 percent of funeral service graduates)?[7]

I started to receive more client referrals from funeral home owners and younger-generation licensees who wanted to become managers or future owners and needed extra support, resources, and coaching. Some were men who reached out, but most were women. And the next thing I knew, I was coaching a group of young people, mostly women, who wanted to grow themselves as future leaders in the deathcare profession.

The postpandemic years were a catalyst for my coaching company and a catalyst for funeral service to perhaps change and wake up to a

---

6   American Board of Funeral Service Education, "For Educators," https://www.abfse.org/html/educators.html.

7   American Board of Funeral Service Education, "For Educators," https://www.abfse.org/html/educators.html.

new reality of a lack of experienced and licensed employee shortages, shrinking profits and death call numbers, and increasing cremation rates. Death call rates along with increasing cremation and other new types of disposition choices are now steadily growing and are not going away; in fact, these disposition choices are predicted to continue to grow in the future in most markets until they reach levels like our profession has never seen. The Cremation Association of North America (CANA) (https://cremationassociation.org) in their annual report predicts that the US national cremation growth rate could exceed 75 percent (possibly 80 percent) as early as 2038. The post-pandemic years gave us a strong message that it was time to change from denial to acceptance of new ways in doing business.

The pandemic changed everything for deathcare and funeral service. Before 2020, we didn't normally have best practices, programs for electronic signatures, and the ability to have meetings consistently on Zoom or Microsoft Teams. Live streaming for funerals, gravesides, or life celebrations was barely being used even though the technology was beginning to be more readily available. Most in funeral service had no ability to show and arrange services online unless they were a progressive firm or cremation society. Face time, phone calls, and faxes were how most in funeral service did business. Some had neither interactive websites nor electronic death certification. Funeral service was more than ten—and, in some cases, twenty—years behind contemporary businesses today. Thus, the majority of smaller firms in the United States went through a lot of new learning, changes, heartache, and loss during the pandemic year and the years following. Now, we are hearing from those who speak to us at conferences that a growing number of employees are struggling with some long-term mental health issues, including compassion fatigue and burnout.

The suicide rate has increased for the general public since the pandemic. The National Center for Health Statistics reported in a data brief that suicide is one of the leading causes of death in the United States.[8] Rates declined a bit between 2018 and 2020, but after the pandemic, they returned to their peak numbers in 2022. The elderly in 2022 were the most severely affected, and behind them the 45–54-year-olds, followed by the 25–34-year-olds. Although we don't have data on our own profession at this time, many of us hear the stories from our profession and especially from psychologists and thanatologists who are consultants to our profession—such as Alan Wolfelt, PhD (https://www .centerforloss.com), and Sara Murphy, PhD, death educator, suicidologist, and fellow in thanatology (https://www.deathdoc .com)—who speak to us at various funeral, cremation, and cemetery conferences on compassion fatigue and burnout in the profession. They also share with us how to help both those who are struggling in the profession and families whose loved ones died by suicide. Death by suicide is real, and we need to pay more attention to the mental health of those who work in deathcare daily. As we speak to each other at meetings, we are hearing that we all have been touched by suicide or know someone in funeral service who has died by suicide.

More than ever before, we need to take better care of ourselves in this profession, and as employers, we must really focus on our staffing teams to ensure they are receiving what they need in the areas of mental health and wellness. I believe, most especially in these postpandemic years, in the need to pay more attention to the people who work on the front lines, especially those who are under stress, day in and day out, serving those who mourn and those who are dying tragic deaths. Employers must do more; they must spend

---

8 CDC.gov, "Suicide Data and Statistics," October 29, 2024, https://www.cdc.gov/suicide/facts/data.html.

more time with their staff, listening and asking them what they can do to help, empower, coach, mentor, and support them. During the beginning of the pandemic, Gallup reported that feelings of engagement and well-being in the workplace went up in large percentages. But in their more recent *State of the Global Workplace* report, released in 2024, Gallup states that employee engagement stagnated starting in 2023 and overall employee well-being is on the decline.[9] The lack of improvement since the pandemic is showing that employees continue to struggle in their work and in their life, and only 23 percent are engaged and feeling good about their work.

I find it sad that caregiving professionals, such as those in funeral service and deathcare, whose primary role is to take care of people who are mourning, cannot seem to care as much for their own staff as they do for their client families. Perhaps more research should be done in our profession and compared to the Gallup research to see how we measure up as a profession going forward.

I believe that there also needs to be increased leadership efforts in advocating for funeral service to have its own wake-up call regarding employee well-being and job satisfaction, especially postpandemic, with more emotional support, mentorship, and coaching programs.

With all these changes and challenges within our profession, I felt a strong call to be part of the solution. Therefore, I started dreaming and designing what Your Funeral Coach could and would do once the pandemic was over.

As the world opened up again, I started doing speaking engagements on the value of mentoring, employee engagement, and development programs, and I encouraged owners to begin

---

9   Gallup, *State of the Global Workplace: 2024 Full Report*, Gallup Workplace, https://www.gallup.com/workplace/349484/state-of-the-global-workplace.aspx.

establishing employee think tanks and fun-in-the-workplace programs, like I had done when I owed Baue's. I started teaching about mentoring, why it's important, and how it can help staff members feel engaged and valued. These programs seemed to be well accepted, considering that most owners and managers did not know how to be mentors or how to set up mentorship programs in their companies.

I believe it all comes back to needing to take better care of our people. As owners, we spend so much energy focused on finding and retaining our customer base—creating a continuous cycle of retaining clients. But we don't focus on a continuous cycle of caring for and retaining staff. Instead, we put them on a schedule working ten days in a row, working nights and holidays, and they burn out in a few years. Since the majority coming into the profession now are women, it will be women who will primarily have these extra emotional support challenges, especially if they are not well accepted, developed, mentored, or coached. Since founding Your Funeral Coach, I have discovered that women overall still do not seem to have a great deal of support in our profession. We are still in the minority in leadership roles both nationwide and locally in the profession. The women I meet at conferences, along with those I coach, tell me they are experiencing a lack of support and development along with other struggles in various areas of their careers and lives.

The pandemic did not help us overall as a gender in our profession. Many women had children or elderly parents to also care for at home—and during times when they also had to work from home. And those who worked in the direct-service areas, like funeral homes, crematories, and cemetery companies, had to go in to work, wearing masks and protective hazmat gear, and work with families and decedents daily. The families were mourning, and in many instances, they were not allowed to have services or be able to see their loved ones before or after they died. Their anger was often directed toward those in our profession. Funeral directors and embalmers, their transport teams, and all the front-liners had, in my opinion, as hard a job as those in the medical and emergency field did. Death was even affecting them personally. I still hear their stories of their own personal losses, of friends and family who did not survive COVID, and, at the same time, how hard it was for them to help others during that time. One of our funeral directors contracted COVID from a family she served, and her elderly parent, who lived with her, contracted it and died very soon thereafter. Funeral directors did their very best to protect themselves, but sometimes, the end result was very difficult and affected them deeply and personally.

Are they still dealing with the effects of the pandemic? I believe many are, and if they remain in our profession, they could use our help and support as colleagues. I have heard many funeral-home owners share that because the pandemic was more than five years ago, stress, burnout, and compassion fatigue are things they are tired of hearing about. How sad is that? I believe we as a profession are responsible for these continued challenges with employees' mental health and that we can do better as a profession, as owners and managers, both now and in the future. If not, I fear we will continue to have more and more retention problems.

Women especially may still be feeling the long-term effects of the pandemic. They share with me that they are (there are, of course, exceptions) feeling neither supported overall nor understood. The younger generation that is now entering the profession is having many of the same concerns, most especially with the lack of development and the challenging schedules that leave little time for self-care. They are beginning to question whether this is the right profession for them. I hear their stories every time I am with them, and it seems those concerns are growing. These younger professionals are being told by their managers and owners, "This is just the way it is. Get used to it, or leave." Or, "If you want to be in leadership, you better not want to have children." Is this okay? No, it is not okay that you cannot have a good work–life balance, get married, have children if you want to, or have a life outside the office in the deathcare profession. But in order to achieve balance, changes must be made in how we do business, and these changes need to happen soon, or we risk losing a large generation of skilled workers and compassionate caregivers, the majority of them women!

LEADERSHIP AS A WOMAN

As I wrote this chapter, I was returning from a Professional Women's Conference sponsored by the National Funeral Directors Association, where my family's charitable fund is now providing more than twenty scholarships a year, in honor of my dad, to help women attend. In 2024, this conference had 175 women attending from all roles—operators of businesses, newer licensees, suppliers, sales teams, and senior leaders in our profession. We came together to support each other and grow; it was wonderful. However, even though twenty-plus women received these scholarships, more than ninety had applied, which means that seventy-plus women may not have been able to attend. Women are seeking more, wanting more in connection and support from the profession, and more must be done.

Conferences are where I hear from so many women about their challenges. Many who attended conferences in 2021 to 2024 are scholarship recipients and told me they had to take PTO days or vacation time just to be there, because their employers would not pay their way or help them with any financial assistance to attend. What is sad is that these women love this profession, but it seems that the large majority are not feeling loved or respected in return, as professionals, as funeral directors, or as women.

I have been through the gamut of feelings of not being loved, not respected, and not taken seriously in funeral service in my forty-four-year career (as of 2025). In my early years, I could not travel alone without my husband or have dinner with a male professional colleague or supplier without people whispering that I was having an affair with someone. In my own community, there were those who thought Baue would fail with a woman in charge. They frequently spread rumors that we were failing and selling, because they assumed Lisa couldn't make it without her dad or husband to help her.

When I was a pregnant and nursing mother, there were those who thought I should have stayed home or retired for a number of years. They said pregnant women should not be working funerals or take fifteen-minute breaks to pump so we could have milk for our babies that night. When I was pregnant with my second child and daughter, I was two weeks from delivering, and a good friend's dad had just died. I was on part-time bedrest because I had swollen ankles. I was not going to miss her dad's funeral. After all, she was pregnant, too, and due the week after me. To this day, when I see her (our daughters grew up together and became fast friends), we laugh at how plump and swollen we were as we waddled down the aisle, holding on to each other. And then we hug and cry, remembering her dad and mine and how we lost them way too young. This is what we do as funeral directors, and as we look back, we have no regrets—only a sense that we did the right thing by being present for those who mourn.

It used to really upset me—being criticized, doubted, or not being taken seriously. Yet it's highly likely one of the reasons I strove so hard to succeed: to prove all of the naysayers wrong.

I've experienced many instances of discrimination on a local, state, and national level, and I am hearing from many whom I coach that this discrimination is still going on today. We do not, as a profession, have statistics about the number of women who have been in leadership positions in the profession's history. I am finding that some associations track them but some do not. Many of them have women leaders and women constituting the majority of their staff. The National Funeral Directors Association (NFDA) currently has CEO Christine Pepper as head of their association. Three other purposed national and international associations located in the United States—the Cremation Association of North America (CANA), the International Cemetery, Cremation and Funeral Association (ICCFA), and the Order of the Golden Rule (OGR)—also have female leadership as their executive directors—Barbara Kemmis, Nadira Baddeliyanage, and Wendy King, respectively—and these associations have also had women in their president's chair a few times. OGR is the clear winner, with five women who have served as their board chairs, yet in all of their histories, this has been more of an exception than a norm.

My guess is that if we researched all the national and state associations in the entire profession, we would find a very small percentage have been elected to the boards or have gone up the chairs into leadership. Is this discrimination? Or are women smaller in numbers in the current generations and just have not been able to serve yet or are not being supported or encouraged? I am fairly certain it is a combination of all of these. I hear from many of my younger female clients that this is still a good ol' boys' club in most of their states. This is beginning to change slowly, and I hope it will change even more in the years to come, when our profession finds a better balance of men and women working together for its betterment.

I can't tell you the number of times I experienced—and the women I have coached still tell me they've experienced—being ignored, not taken seriously, harassed, bullied, or seen as a sexual object instead of a professional. Sometimes for me, the harassment was sexual in nature, with advancements from men older than and the same age as me. I have been solicited by international, national, and state leaders; men who were married; and men who were single. None of it was okay with me. I was appalled, upset, and at times felt like I would never gain men's respect. I did my best to reject their offers in a professional way, because that is how I was raised: to always behave respectfully, like a professional. As I aged, however, I found myself growing less and less tolerant of this type of behavior from the men in my profession, especially from those in my own generation.

In retrospect, you might wonder why I cared. I cared because it hurt. It always hurt to feel unsupported, criticized, and disrespected. It hurts now to watch other women go through this as well, especially because we were and are all trying to do our best to be good leaders with little support and few role models. In my case, I was doing all I could to take leadership courses, reading leadership books, and hiring a leadership coach so that I could grow myself to be better, provide growth for my staff, and better serve the families in our community. My leadership coach taught me to let a lot of these negative things roll off my shoulders over the years and continue to present myself in the best professional manner. Sometimes, however, it was a little harder than I could handle.

One difficult instance had to do with my dream to serve as the first woman leader of a national association in our profession. I had served before as a president of an organization midway through my career for a funeral service marketing association, and it was a wonderful experience. I was not the first woman president, and it didn't matter because I was accepted by both men and women. Women were easily accepted in this group—in part, I believe, because of the executive director, Marilyn Gould, who provided excellent leadership—and many of the men became very close friends of mine.

Toward the end of my career, I still had this dream of wanting to become a woman leader of another organization that had been near and dear to my heart during my career. This organization's membership included some of my mentors and best friends in the profession and was a big part of my early career's success. I wanted to give back and be a good role model to other women who were starting to join in larger numbers.

Over the years, I'd had to turn this group down a couple of times when they requested I serve on their board. At those times, my family priorities had taken precedence, but later in life, I had a chance to serve again and ran for president. We had a tie, so the board votes continued a couple of times, and then eventually, the tie was broken. I was not voted to serve as what would have been this organization's first woman president.

One individual who voted against me that day was someone I thought was a professional friend, who said he had my back and then, for some reason at the end, didn't. I tried hard not to take it personally, because my heart was broken and I loved this association. So I put on my best professional face that day and congratulated the winner, a man who had been a friend over the years from my own generation. He was and still is a good guy, and he became a good president. I promised to serve as his supporter and partner on the board for the betterment of the association because it was the right thing to do.

The real struggle I was having was in discovering that some-one I thought was a friend—someone who I supported and had thought supported me in return—had not been honest with me. He changed his vote and was never truthful. That is what hurt the most. After a few weeks, I decided to have a conversation with him. He continued to deny that his was the vote that changed. Yet I knew from others this was not true. Those who know me well know that honesty is one of my core values. Respect is another. When someone crosses those lines, I lose respect for them and can no longer trust them. Trust in friendships and business relationships is huge to me, and I know it is to most people in this profession. It is pretty much my line in the sand.

After a good hearty cry and allowing my insecurities and self-doubt to creep in again to tell me I was not good enough, I realized that some people are so self-serving and dishonest with others that they will not change, and it wasn't really about me. This experience was the end of our friendship. It was also another wake-up call for me in being more careful in who I chose and trusted as friends.

That next year, as I served on the board, the president and other board members helped the organization with their next strategic plan. In this work, I strove to be the best role model and mentor I could be for the other women in our association who still needed my help. It was important work. I had to put aside my hurt feelings and my ego (yes, we all have a little) that in some ways wanted to be "the first" and lead by example. I needed to show other women to not give up and to continue to serve in leadership positions, no matter the official role or title. I needed to continue to serve for the greater good of the association and the profession and feel I was always giving it my best. How often have women done this in our history of working women? I think the history books are full of women who have sacrificed their roles for the sake of the greater good. It is the right thing to do always, albeit at times frustrating.

As I write this chapter, we've just come through another national election for president of the United States. Twice now, our country has not elected a woman as president. Politics aside—and please know this is not a statement nor an endorsement for a person or one particular party over the other—to me, it's becoming obvious that it takes time for women in any profession to ascend to the top leadership role. The glass ceiling still exists for women in business and in politics. I do hope to live to see the day when this is no longer the case. However, at this rate, it will more than likely be my granddaughters' generation that will experience more equity in the workplace and in leadership roles.

It's sad but still true that today in the funeral service and deathcare profession, there are still men who do not treat women well. I don't want to point fingers totally at my generation of Baby Boomer colleagues, but unfortunately, many of the offenders whom I hear about from those I coach are still in ownership or leadership. It is my hope that other generations are becoming wiser and are more supportive of women and diverse members of other minority communities, as these are the people coming into our workplace in the largest numbers. They deserve to be treated with respect, dignity, and acceptance. This next era of leaders wants and needs to be developed, engaged, coached, and mentored. They deserve to know that their employers truly do care for their well-being. And they deserve to grow as leaders, with the ability to use their heads, their grit, and most especially the incredible hearts they bring to funeral service each and every day.

The struggles I've faced in this profession as a woman are not unique just to me. I hear similar stories from the women I network with and whom I coach each and every time we are together. I also hear beautiful stories filled with their dreams and goals for their future. They are not sure how to get to where they want to be someday, which is why they reach out for coaching. Some want to be owners, some want to be managers, and some just want to be treated respectfully and fairly by those they work with or for. Many lack belief in themselves and self-confidence. They have a hard time finding their voices and standing up for themselves, especially to those in higher authority. Some feel they have been passed over for opportunities or enticed into working for someone who has promised them ownership or management positions but then let them down. Many are becoming discouraged and fear our profession will never change, never accept them fully, and never allow them to become leaders, owners, or managers. Many have been disenchanted, neither trained nor developed in ways they believe they need to be successful.

Yet they have a strong desire to succeed and love our profession so much. These women have wonderful hearts and have been trying to use them in all they do in their careers, but at times, their hearts have been hurt. Along with women, I hear of many from the LGBTQ+ community and different minority group members, who are also facing additional challenges in our profession today. They are seeking acceptance and in rare cases are finding it. I say "rare" because the majority of the time, they tell me that they are not feeling accepted totally or respected. This is just so sad to me.

All of us in funeral service need to do better, be better, put our prejudices aside, and accept them. After all, we accept the families we serve, don't we? We do not turn families away because of who they are, what they look like, and what their beliefs are, do we? No! Then why are we rejecting—instead of supporting, training, and developing—employees from these groups, both men and women?

I believe that if our profession wakes up and begins to embrace, empower, and better support women and diverse workforces entering our profession, we can and will be better. We will not just survive; we will begin to thrive and grow as individuals, as businesses, and as a profession.

Self-Reflection Questions

- When you are at an impasse in life and are unsure of what to do, who do you turn to for guidance? What was their advice, and how did you act on it?

- Does the difficulty inherent in the profession wear on you? Do you feel like you're mostly able to leave it at work, or do you bring it home with you? How can you take extra care of yourself on those days?

- Do you think women are afforded truly equal opportunity in this profession? In what ways do you see room to improve? In what ways can you become more involved in leadership areas?

10

The Little Dead Girl
and Hope for the Future

I love this profession, alongside all its difficulties, and all of the mysteries it brings us close to. I first came into closest proximity with its mysteries when I was ten years old. I had just tiptoed into the funeral parlor that held the casketed body of a young girl about the same age as me. The air smelled of flowers, some fragrant, some overwhelmingly sweet.

I had snuck in quietly, because I knew I wasn't supposed to be there. My dad had told me earlier in the day not to go in that room, but I was way too curious. Besides, since he'd told me not to go in, I had to wonder, *Why can't I?* I'd seen dead people before, including my own grandparents. *So*, I thought, *why can't I just take a peek?*

As I approached the casket, I saw this little girl, and except for her brown hair, it felt like I was looking in the mirror. She looked like me. Her dress was light pink, and the room was filled with all different kinds of fragrant flowers, mostly pink, some white and yellow. It seemed that she was just asleep. I thought she looked so pretty and peaceful. How could she possibly be dead?

I found myself just staring at her for a few minutes. Although I'd never touched a dead person before, I wanted to touch her, maybe to comfort her, maybe to comfort me, and maybe as a way to mourn and acknowledge her young death. I slowly reached out and touched her crepe dress, her little cross necklace, and the cross with beads around her hands. I touched her fingers and her hand. I found that she was cold, very cold, and her skin had makeup on it that came off on my hands. As I saw this, I hoped I had not messed the makeup up because I knew that I would then be in big trouble with my dad.

Back then, I did not really know what grieving was, but I felt my eyes getting watery and a tear slowly slid down my cheek. I didn't know this little girl, but I was sad for her and so very sad for her family, who were now going to have to live without her. As I quietly left the parlor (thankfully unnoticed), I realized that I had no one to tell about my experience of the little dead girl. My girlfriends would think it was too creepy. I had disobeyed my dad and couldn't tell him, and I knew my mom, too, would be furious if she found out and never leave me alone in the funeral home again. So who could I talk to?

Without anyone to share the experience with, I went outside for some fresh air and to think for a bit. As I sat down on the front doorstep of the funeral home entrance, I remember looking up to the sky, trying to compose myself and silently asking God why little girls had to die. I'm not sure he answered me at that moment, but right after I asked him this question, I heard the front door open behind me and my dad's deep voice asking me what I was doing out there. I stood up quickly, wiped the tears from my eyes, and turned to face my father. I said I was just enjoying the nice day and waiting for Mom to come pick me up after school. Since I went to school across the street, I was thinking it was really a semi-honest answer, right?

I could then see in my dad's eyes that he knew I had been in to see the little dead girl, and perhaps the makeup I still had on my hands had made it up to my own face, too. Dad didn't say another word. He slowly smiled. Then, he put his arm around me and led me inside to wait for my mom. My dad and I never talked about that little girl again, but I knew he could somehow see how I was feeling. Dad didn't get mad at me for disobeying him. In fact, I'd like to think that my dad could see that I had felt some sympathy for the young girl and her family. Perhaps he could see that I had something inside of me, something that I was going to need as I grew into a young adult and perhaps one day became a compassionate funeral director.

I think for both of us, that little dead girl experience was a profound moment: He might have started considering me then for the future of our family business, and it planted a seed for my eventually realizing this work was something I could do and do well. Little did I know at the time that the feeling of sadness for the little girl and her family was a sympathetic moment and a key skill that I would need later on in life. Today, though, I can see, looking back, how it was a defining moment for me in understanding the caring needed to serve others as they experienced that death of a loved one, especially a child. I believe it was an experience that spoke to me later in my adult life, when I realized that I could be a compassionate funeral director who cared deeply when someone experiences a death in their lives.

SYMPATHY AND EMPATHY

Back when I first began meeting with families as a funeral director, I became the children and infant funeral director. It's not that the others, all men, couldn't do it; they could. Perhaps, though, they somehow thought that I was more suited to meeting with these families, or perhaps it was too painful for them to deal with, and thought, *We will just let the woman director do it.* I may never know the real reason they wanted me to meet the majority of these types of families. What I did know is that I was there to serve families and believed that if I could make a difference in their lives, if I could touch their hearts with kindness and sympathy, I would have done all I needed to.

One day, a call came on my cell phone from a friend of mine, who shared with me that her nephew had just died after a short battle with leukemia at age eleven. Would I meet with her, her sister, and her sister's husband the next day? I said of course I would.

After the arrangements were complete, I received a call that the young boy was in our care, so I could go see him. Usually, I always tried to see the individual who died before I met the family, but in this circumstance, it was not possible, and I did not see him until later in the day. Perhaps God knows what he is doing, or perhaps it's coincidence, but for whatever reason, in this case, I was grateful, because when I saw him, I realized that this young boy looked exactly like my son, John. And I mean he looked *exactly* like my son, with the same nose, eyelashes, high cheekbones, lips, and ears. I had to do a double take; their features were so similar. Except for his light brown hair, this boy could have been my son, and they were the same age—eleven years old.

I sobbed as I stood there beside him. I held his cold small hand, and I cried for his family. I cried out of fear of the possibility of losing my son to leukemia, too. I really do not remember how long I cried, but it felt like more than an hour. As I left to go home that day, I cried in the car, too, and when I walked in the door to our home, I called for my son. I hugged him, and I cried some more. Only a funeral director who is a parent will fully understand the pain of these moments.

I realized the next day, as I was preparing myself mentally to serve this family, that I needed to have more time with my son. I told my then-husband Michael that I was taking him with me on the ride to Illinois to conduct the funeral and graveside. While he tried to understand, and although he was a funeral director, too, he was questioning whether my plan was wise, and he asked me who I was doing this for. Michael was right—it was for me—but I felt I needed John with me that day as a reminder that he was okay and I was okay, too. So I compromised. I called my cousin in Illinois and asked her whether John could stay that day with her and her daughter until I was finished with the funeral.

As I drove the hearse that Saturday the hour and a half to my cousin's hometown, my son and I chatted about life, death, and the little boy in the back of the hearse. John had a lot of questions. He had not been to a funeral since he had turned four, when my dad died, and he didn't remember a lot. Over the years, I have asked John if he remembers that day when he rode in the hearse to Illinois with me and the little dead boy, and he does vaguely, but not in detail. Yet I certainly do.

I remember the comfort it gave to me to have him with me that day. I remember his questions about death, about leukemia, about funerals. Our conversation helped ground me and better serve the little boy's family with sympathy, not empathy. Sympathy is understanding someone else's suffering, and empathy is beginning to feel what the other person is feeling, which is a tough place for a funeral director to be in. It can tear you up over time, from the inside out. In fact, I think for some funeral directors who cannot stay in sympathy mode, at least most of the time, this may be part of why they experience burnout early or even later in their careers.

As the day came to a close and I was debriefing the funeral at my cousin's house, I realized that keeping the deaths of children in perspective is never easy. This was an occurrence in which it was hard to stay within the bounds of deep caring and sympathy. I also realized that I am human and that serving a family can hit very close to home sometimes. That day, while I conducted the funeral in Illinois, there was a point when I had to walk out from the back of church, take a big breath, cry a few tears, and look up in the sky and ask God, *Why do young children have to die?*

I think I finally understood in that moment why my dad hadn't gotten mad at me all those years ago when he realized I had disobeyed him and gone to seen the little dead girl. I would like to believe that it was because he saw something in me that let him know I had a heart for this work. He also knew that we do not always find the answers to our questions, especially about all the tragic deaths we deal with as funeral directors. Sometimes, these deaths will hurt our hearts, too, and we must be able to dig down deep inside ourselves and be able to handle these tough times, using our grit.

As far as answers from God about why children die, I'll leave that up to him to tell us someday. He doesn't always give us the immediate answers, but he does know how to put us in the right place at the right time so we can use our strengths and grit combined with our hearts in caring for the families of children who have died. I've been in these places many times over my life in funeral service since that funeral, and although it was never easy, I knew that I had the ability to do it as often as needed.

GETTING TO WORK

This profession can be difficult. Yet if you love it and you feel the capacity in yourself to meet others with compassion without drowning in their grief, I encourage you not to give up on it. In our work, we create a sacred space that helps people mourn well, and we walk with them through some of the most difficult times of their lives.

Our work is also challenging. You will experience your own grief, you will cry, you will feel like sometimes you did not make a difference. You will have families get angry with you and blame you for something that goes wrong, and you will feel you let them down. When that happens, apologize, and try to make it right and better for them always. We know from experience and from studying grief that when families are mourning, they can be unlike their normal selves. Do your best not to take it personally, and always show them your heart and that you care.

Do the same for your fellow team members. Remember that all of you are going to have hard days, and you can all be leaders in helping each other survive and thrive through them. No matter what, love them all, care for them all, and continue to be the best and most helpful team member you can be. Through it all, show them your heart.

Also, care for yourself. This business will take its toll on you and wear you out some days, weeks, and months. Mental and physical self-care is essential to surviving and thriving into the future. So is advocating for yourself. In my coaching work, I spend a lot of time helping those I coach, especially women, develop their grit, their self-confidence, and their resilience. I focus on teaching them how to cope with the hard times and bad days, how to learn to have the difficult conversations and ask for what they need and deserve. You may be asking yourself, "What about the men? Don't they have heart, too?" Of course they do, and I know of so many compassionate caregiving men in our profession. Yet men are often raised and treated differently from women, and because of this, they tend to interact with the world differently. I see this all of this quite clearly in funeral service and have focused my work on helping women grow as leaders, in the face of their many challenges.

As a woman in deathcare today, it is highly likely that you will need to seek help outside of your current employment in order to grow yourself as a leader and become more comfortable being gritty and resilient. You must find a place of inner courage and inner strength where you can then use your mind and heart to let employers know what you need—whether that's training, development, or work–life balance—and then advocate for it in a professional, caring, confident way. And once you are in leadership, it's essential you continue to use your head, your heart, and grit to conduct yourself and support your team and your business in a compassionate, courageous, effective manner.

I learned how to do this through a series of profound wake-up calls and from my mentors and coaches I had throughout my life, along with doing a ton of book reading on business and leadership. These pivot points helped me learn how to be smarter and use my head. They helped me learn to persevere with courage. And, most importantly, they helped me learn that the heart needed in my leadership style was to first and foremost help my own people. These wake-up calls taught me how to be a better person overall, how to treat others with more care and respect, how to put my staff first and foremost at work, and last but not least, they taught me how to find the work–life balance that I deserved, that the people in my life deserved, and that the staff at Baue deserved.

Throughout all of our lives, we each have wake-up calls. My question to you is this: Are you listening to them? Learning from them? Working to get better for them? Are you finding others, like mentors and coaches, to help you with them?

Are you wondering where to find them? I hope this book will help you find the answers.

Many of these wake-up calls—well, most of them—are hard and can be life-changing. They *should* be life-changing. Death is hard, grief is hard, and working in the deathcare profession is hard. Being a funeral director, embalmer, sales professional, manager, or owner is hard. No matter what your role, working in and around death every day of your career is not easy, but in the long run, realizing you are making a difference in people's lives lifts you up and helps you feel a sense of pride in what you do. Being a wife, a mother, a family member, and a friend while being around death daily can be hard. Being authentic and honest with ourselves when life and work gets hard is difficult too. We must reach out for help, seek advice, and find others we trust and can rely on to talk to about how we are feeling. No matter how many times we fall, fail, or feel that we can't go on, we must remember to use our hearts, our minds, and our grit to support ourselves and others. We must seek to find fulfillment in our life's work, discovering the best place for us to be both in our personal life and our careers. Regardless of all the things in our lives that go wrong or go right, we must be true to ourselves, our personal values, and our purpose and mission.

Being a leader is difficult, and it takes work to become one. We are helping to take care of others, and that's never going to be an easy job. It's imperative if we wish to lead people—whatever our current title or role—that we develop our minds, rely on our grit to push through, and use our hearts in all we do. If you are in the beginning of your career, be patient with yourself. Funeral service and all jobs in the deathcare profession take time to learn, so if you are passionate about the profession, become a lifelong learner. Read all you can, both online and in books. Seek to attend professional meetings. Seek out scholarships from organizations to get out in the field to learn even more. If you identify as a woman, connect with us at the Funeral Women Lead Foundation, and explore the training we offer through the leadership academy and our coaching and mentoring programs along with our wellness summit and our supportive community. Discover women's groups and programs in our profession and in your own area. If there are not any, consider starting one. And remember that you can connect with the Funeral Women Lead Foundation online and by scanning the QR code at the back of this book.

If your employer does not provide opportunities for development, sit down with them and ask them to do so. Tell them why it is important to you and how it will benefit them! If that does not work, find ways to develop yourself, or perhaps find another employer, so you have a variety of experiences to learn from. As a woman or a member of a diverse community, learning to advocate and believe in yourself even in the face of discouragement is essential.

Learn to set SMART goals and work–life balance goals for yourself. Know you can achieve anything you put your mind to. It will take patience, perseverance, fortitude, and hard, smart work. It will take giving your time and talents—and some of your nights and weekends. Although we all deserve to have a better work–life balance, this is not a Monday-to-Friday nine-to-five business. It is, though, a business that can give you a great deal of meaning and satisfaction.

You must be yourself and discover what you really want in life. If it is the deathcare profession, then give it your all, regardless of the current role you are in now. You will have failures, make mistakes, fall, get up, and fall again. You'll make decisions that don't result in what you thought they would. If you are an owner or become an owner, you will have people in your employment leave, come and go, and maybe even become untrustworthy. You will have haters and naysayers who want to see you fail. If you're a woman or a member of a diverse group, you'll face additional challenges as this profession slowly and belatedly moves its way out of the twentieth century and into an era of further equity and inclusion. Your resilience will be essential. It can carry you through. Your mind will be valuable. Fill it with wise counsel and learning. Your heart will make all the difference. Keep it open and share it.

You will have times you will be afraid. If that happens, here is a little missive that I like to share that is based on Kent Keith's poem "Do It Anyway" and a similar poem written by Mother Teresa:

A Few Words to Help You Remain Strong and Find Your Grit

If you are faced with self-doubt and you
want to quit, lift yourself up anyway.
If you are struggling in your education
and you feel way behind, continue to learn anyway.
If you want to defend yourself and your heart has
been hurt, remain strong, and open your heart anyway.
If you want to succeed and you
need real support, seek help anyway.
If you seek to become a leader but feel you have nowhere to turn,
seek others to teach you, and become a leader anyway.
If you feel your voice has been silenced
and you have something to say, speak up anyway.
If you are not sure whether you will ever
reach your dream, keep reaching for it anyway.

I've experienced all of the above and have pushed through the tough times and tried and tried to be successful and a better person anyway. Those who know me best will tell you that I do not give up easily. I did not always do things perfectly, but through listening to my wake-up calls, I learned, and I grew. I woke up to being true to myself, to loving and living my passion of caring deeply and helping people who are in true need. And now I have found truly fulfilling work, through my coaching and my foundation, that allows me to help others, especially women in my profession, to become successful and make a difference. Why do I do this? Why didn't I just retire completely and ride off on my horse into the sunset like in the movies? (I do love to ride my horse.)

I do this because I still believe there is work to do to help our profession be better. I do this because I want to help others who are newer and growing in our profession find the help they need. And I do it because I was raised to help others. When I was a new funeral director, my dad encouraged me to join the Jaycees. In my twenties, it had a profound impact on my growing as a young adult after college and was a good beginning to my leadership journey, joining with a group of young people my age in the community learning how to put on projects that benefited our community. One Jaycee creed teaches us, "Service to humanity is the best work of life!" This is etched now into the granite in my family's mausoleum and has always been in my heart since I joined this service club. Helping others and my profession has been built into my DNA. It's who I am. It's my mission in life. And I'm so grateful for all the mentors, coaches, team members, professional friends, and family who've supported me during my lifelong leadership journey.

As I end my message, I would say this especially to the women along with those from diverse communities working in funeral service: Please don't give up on our profession. If you have the heart for it, if you have a personality that can bring compassion yet not fully take on the grief of others, if you're willing to seek support as needed to swim hard through heavy waves and care for yourself at the same time, if it calls to you—it's worth the difficult times and the many challenges. Working in deathcare isn't for everyone, but for those of us called to it, we're a part of something deeply meaningful and irreplaceable as we give support and comfort to those we serve. We walk with people through some of the hardest times in their lives by offering care and compassion that gives them a space to grieve and mourn as they need to. This work matters, your work matters, and you matter!

The profession must change in how it cares for and develops its staff so we can continue doing this incredibly necessary work in the right way, and it needs all of our help to do so. We need you to speak up, and keep speaking up *anyway* by using your heart, your head, and your grit. If your employer isn't responsive, start looking for one who will be. And if you love this profession as much as I do, I really encourage you to stay strong and begin the path of starting to develop yourself as a leader. However supportive your employer is or isn't, keep trying, and don't give up.

If you don't know where to start, first, find a mentor in the profession or a leadership coach, someone you admire and look up to. Look for organizations that will help support you; they are out there and can be found with a Google search.

As of this writing, some of the state and national organizations are beginning to provide more supportive mentoring and leadership programs, and we are seeing more women's support programs, too.

- The National Funeral Directors Association (NFDA.org) and its charitable arm, the Funeral Service Foundation (funeralservicefoundation.org), with its scholarship programs, can greatly help you. Its annual Professional Women's Conference has great speakers, women's scholarships, and networking opportunities.

- The International Cemetery, Cremation, and Funeral Association (ICCFA.org) has an annual university for higher learning and a women's committee that has grown recently to address members' needs and host programs annually.

- The Cremation Association of North America (cremationassociation.org) has great learnings offered two times a year and offers scholarships along with the Funeral Service Foundation to help you learn more about cremation best leadership practices.

- The Death Care Collective (deathcarecollective.com) has an online book club, mentoring, and webinars and is now, as of the writing of this book, forming regional women's support groups around the United States.

- Continuing Vision (continuingvision.com), a continuing education unit–based online learning program, offers mentoring to new licensees from one to five years licensed.

- Funeral Professionals Peer Support (funeralspeersupport.com) offers peer-based mental wellness and support groups to bereavement professionals.

- Some of the independent associations, such as Selected Independent Funeral Homes (selectedfuneralhomes.org) and the Order of the Golden Rule (OGR.org), are offering leadership development programs and online learning, along with some supportive programs for women.

- And our newly founded **Funeral Women Lead Foundation** (funeralwomenlead.org) provides a hands-on two-year path in our women's leadership academy and an annual wellness summit, along with coaching and mentoring, growing resources, and an online community geared specifically toward women based on their needs to grow themselves as leaders.

- I do my best to stay on top of the current trends in the profession. I offer some blogging, a women's leadership podcast, and a coaching program through the Funeral Women Lead Foundation. You can find me online on all forms of social media and my YouTube channel, and you may also contact me directly at LisaBaue.com to learn more.

I encourage you to do some research and find out what works best for you. I really want to see you apply for the many scholarships that are out there today and to all of the associations and foundations in our profession, including Funeral Women Lead, that will support your continued growth and development. Search for them, and use them to attend as many conferences and conventions as you can.

Explore the many online learning opportunities available through webinars and podcasts in the deathcare industry. Read or listen to all the books, podcasts, webinars, TED Talks, etc., you can on leadership. Take charge of your own learning, and develop yourself into the best leader you can be. If an employer agrees to make you a part of their succession plan, have a crucial conversation, get the plan in writing, and seek the financing you need (it's out there in our profession, from the Small Business Administration and some select other lending sources). We will have many coaches and mentors at Funeral Women Lead to help you find what you need.

Be proactive about your own course. Learn to lead yourself, and learn to also lead others, whatever position you seek to hold in funeral service. None of this happens overnight, but step by step, you can move toward your goals and thrive in our profession. As a growing leader in this profession, whatever your title, you'll experience many rewards. One is knowing that you can make a real difference. As a current or future leader, you can encourage others to grow in their own journey, and you can also make the profession better for the families we serve and all of us who make deathcare our life's work.

Please also remember: As a coach, I see you and hear you. Sing loudly with your "gritty" voice, and speak with your compassionate heart and your smart head, using all three of them in all you do. I stand with you, and there are others out there who will, too. Have hope; draw from your head, your heart, and your grit every day; and keep the faith that you will become the change our profession desperately needs while you also reach toward your goals and dreams!

You can do it. I believe in you!

Now, get out there, believe in yourself and your ability to unleash your greatness, and become a leader—*anyway*!

Self-Reflection Questions

- What three women's support programs can you reach out to this week—or encourage women colleagues to reach out to—to help fuel your (or their) career development?

- What three books, webinars, or podcasts do you want to use to expand your professional skill set this quarter?

- Which three people can you reach out to in search of a professional mentor or coach?

A Note to Current
Leaders in the Profession

First, I want to thank you for coming on this journey with me. If you are already leading in a way that takes care of your own people, first and foremost, I want to congratulate and celebrate you. Thank you so much for being part of the shift and growth that are much needed in this profession. If, instead, you recognize that there is plenty of room for change and improvement in your leadership and in your business, I want to celebrate this moment you are in now, too. The first stage is recognizing there is a need to change; the second is doing something about it. I know firsthand it isn't easy to acknowledge the ways you may not be living up to your highest potential as a current, new, or future leader, and I encourage you to not give up on yourself but embrace a commitment to keep doing better. I'm grateful for my own evolution in this space, and I am grateful for the openness to new learning you are showing through reading this book.

In 2025, we are in a time of transition. What many of us in the Baby Boomer and Gen X generations grew up with in the profession—expectations of how the workplace should operate with their on-duty schedules versus the reality of what it really is, especially in funeral, cremation, and burial companies, with as many as ten consecutive work days in a row and way too many of those nights, weekends, and holidays on call and working; a lack of employee training and development programs; and a lack of empathetic, caring leadership—will no longer cut it. Disrespectful and downright inappropriate treatment of those who are different from us—especially women and various ethnic and other minorities, including members of the LGBTQ+ community, who are in or entering the profession and have not been treated well, acknowledged, developed, or respected—is not okay. The state of the profession, and especially the additional difficulties women and others face, is contributing to compassion fatigue; in some cases, severe burnout; and, some experts believe, an increasing suicide rate—as well as people leaving the profession at numbers higher than we realize. New research is being conducted these next few years to learn more about job satisfaction, engagement, and why employees are leaving deathcare and funeral service to help our profession understand more and continue to help and wake up the employers and managers in our profession who need to change before it's too late.

The worldwide pandemic beginning in 2020 compounded the problem we have today in finding and retaining employees. But I do not believe it is the only cause of our profession's recruitment and retention problems. During the first year of the pandemic and the difficult years that followed, the funeral, cremation, and cemetery profession saw a rapid—virtually overnight—increase in the number of families they served, and it brought many employees and businesses to a breaking point. Staffs were exhausted because their already-demanding work became even more challenging, with increased working hours and a shortage of protective gear as supply chains shut down. They felt the added pressure of supporting grieving families who were not allowed to have viewings or funerals or to be with their loved ones for final goodbyes, even at the graveside or crematory. Owners and managers became exhausted and disillusioned, often wanting to move toward retirement but lacking the staff to support them, replace their positions, or find anyone to buy their firms at a price they could afford to sell for or retire on. In the subsequent years (some of these years we are still in as of this writing), many have seen a decrease in their death rates, an increase in employee resignations, and, for those that remained, increasing job dissatisfaction and engagement.

Although our profession has no compassion fatigue, burnout, or suicide rates at this time, if you take the time to listen to those who are struggling, as I have through my work as a former owner, consultant, and coach, they will tell you their stories with heartache in their voices and with tears in their eyes. Most firms in our profession have lost good staff during and after the pandemic in what has been called the Great Resignation. Even now, five years later, funeral service is continuing to struggle with staff shortages, especially as Baby Boomers are retiring and others are considering leaving the profession due to burnout, poor wages, and feelings of disengagement. Besides those retiring, those who are leaving seem to be mainly coming from the Millennial and Gen Z generations, with the majority being women.

Women and minorities are currently facing many struggles in our profession. And many of the stories I have heard in my time as a coach, leader, and mentor to this next era of women dishearten me and sometimes make my blood boil. I hear their challenges, their heartaches, and far too many stories of verbal abuse, sexual harassment, and a lack of acceptance from male colleagues and bosses. They share stories of employers who appear to not care and of being treated like they are housekeepers, maintenance, and hearse washers instead of licensed graduates who want to contribute their learning and talents to their roles. Don't get me wrong: I understand that we all have to work on the front lines, especially in smaller firms, to do all we can to keep our buildings and fleets clean and shiny and our families well served, but there is a point where this next generation desires to be developed further in areas of leadership skills and learning. In this area, I am hearing that our profession overall is failing to do so by relying on others or national online programs to teach them—which, while a good start, is not the entire answer to employee training, development, and care programs.

Still today, I continue to hear too often stories of how women and others from minority groups are feeling bullied, ignored, overworked, and underpaid. They have told me that they are burned out, stressed, trying to pay off student loans, and often barely surviving financially. They are not feeling supported in being allowed time to care for themselves or their families. They struggle in self-confidence and finding their voice. And they are experiencing a profound lack of development, training, mentoring, and coaching. At the same time, their ideas are being ignored.

Today, the next era of staff rightly expect more work–life balance, most especially those with young families, and the majority of them are women joining the profession. We should not make it impossible to be a leader doing work that we love—and which the world desperately needs—while also raising a family or taking time for ourselves outside of work. In the funeral, cremation, and burial-service profession that we also call deathcare, we need a revitalization of leadership development for the next era of workers in our profession. We need leadership that goes beyond the rigid, top-down ways of the past to connect emotionally and become closer to those we work with. We need to listen and lead with our hearts, our heads, and our grit, and we need to teach others how to do so with patience and kindness. We need to value inclusion and hire a diverse staff that reflects the communities we serve. We need to draw on the power of mentoring, coaching, and personal development to teach and grow the next generation.

For those of you who believe in leadership development, in supporting women and diverse minorities in our profession, thank you for all you have done, and all you will do, to help take our profession forward into the future. Thank you for believing we need to change and for being the change. Our work matters, and our people matter, and I hope we honor them frequently and with a loud voice by helping our essential profession wake up and be all it can be.

Even if it doesn't work right away or the first or second time you try, do it anyway!

Resources and Associations

LISA BAUE—AUTHOR, COACH, PODCASTER

lisa@lisabaue.com

https://www.lisabaue.com

https://www.linkedin.com/in/lisa-baue

https://www.facebook.com/LisaBaueAuthor

https://www.instagram.com/lisabaue_

FUNERAL WOMEN LEAD FOUNDATION

https://www.funeralwomenlead.org

https://www.linkedin.com/company/funeral-women-lead

https://www.facebook.com/FuneralWomenLead

https://www.instagram.com/funeralwomenlead

ASSOCIATIONS

National Funeral Directors Association:
https://www.nfda.org

Funeral Service Foundation:
https://www.funeralservicefoundation.org

International Cemetery, Cremation, and Funeral Association:
https://www.iccfa.com

Cremation Association of North America:
https://www.cremationassociation.org

Selected Independent Funeral Homes:
https://www.selectedfuneralhomes.org

Order of the Golden Rule:
https://www.ogr.org

Southern Cemetery, Cremation, and Funeral Association:
https://www.sccfa.info

Funeral Service Association of Canada:
https://www.fsac.ca

ADDITIONAL GROUPS AND RESOURCES

Funeral Women Lead:
https://www.funeralwomenlead.org

Death Care Collective:
https://www.deathcarecollective.com

Continuing Vision:
https://www.continuingvision.com

Funeral Professionals Peer Support:
https://www.funeralspeersupport.com

American Board of Funeral Service Education:
https://www.abfse.org

Gallup, Inc.:
https://www.gallup.com

Acknowledgments

I would like to thank Greenleaf Book Group, River Grove Books, and their great team for all their help with publishing, editing, designing the book cover, and getting my story out into the world. To Justin Branch and his team for believing in my story and that the world needs to read it, to Adrianna Hernandez for keeping me on track with a schedule and gentle reminders, to Emma Watson and her team for helping me shore up the title, to Amanda Ellysse Hughes and Meilee Bridges for their final edits and a few rewrites (here and there, LOL), to Hannah Marlow for her work on the book cover, and to all on the Greenleaf and River Grove team of proofers and editors, especially for their faith in me as a first-time author, which helped get my book to market.

A huge shout-out and a sincere *obrigada* to Stacy Ennis (https://www.stacyennis.com), my writing and book coach, published author and founder of the most amazing book-coaching school ever! To my editing and developmental coach and rewriting partner Robin Bethel, your patience in helping me get to the finish line is nothing short of amazing. In times when I was ready to give up or doubted myself as a storyteller and writer, neither of you let me quit. We had a few delays (on my part), because of various travels and the death of my brother, but still you never gave up on me. Your connectedness, staying in touch, and belief in me when I was not sure I could tell all my truths in my story, especially the hard ones, were gifts you have given me that I will never forget and for which I will always be grateful to you both. You truly care for your authors and everyone you coach. You both are amazing role models for me as I continue to coach in the profession and design new programs to help women succeed. Thank you from the bottom of my heart—*o coração*!

To the founding board and staff of Funeral Women Lead, who have been so very supportive and helpful as we launched the foundation at the same time as I was completing the book. You are all friends and trusted professionals—John Schmitz, CPA; Alicia Carr, owner of Kelco Supply; Melissa Posey Loose, senior VP of communications for Security National; and my small but mighty staff: my daughter-in-law, Taylor Crabbs, and Dr. Ruth Bedell. You worked tirelessly to ensure that my vision to help women unleash their greatness would come true with your hard and incredible work!

To my group of trusted advisors at RG Fowler CPA, Cynthia Smith at City Park Legal, Root + River Branding, Oxy.co web designers, and Acropolis Investments. Chris Lissner and Kaley Pogrelis, thank you for answering the call, your support, your heavy lifting, and your diligence in helping my author brand come to life and, at the same time, never giving up on me and my legacy goal to launch Funeral Women Lead in 2024.

To the many clients and mentees of Your Funeral Coach, you know who you are! It has been an honor and privilege to work with you in these last four years. I have learned so much from you. This book and the future of Funeral Women Lead would not exist without meeting you, hearing your stories and your heartaches, and watching you grow and succeed. I am so proud of you all! You have inspired my passion for serving and supporting women even more, especially the next era of managers and owners, who would not exist without you in it.

A special shout-out to Julie, Allyse, Beth, Rachel, Madison, Jennifer, and Joey. You are the future of this profession; you have unleashed and will continue to unleash your greatness. Listen to and use your heart, your grit, and your head in all you do. I will be cheering you on always!

To those whom I have worked with over the years in the profession—my mentors and coaches—from Larry Beeson of the Leaders Network and Marguerite Ham of Igniting Success (https://www.margueriteham.com) to my early women mentors, Anna Louise Bongiovi and Sandra Strong-Fitzgerald, and my very first funeral boss and coach, Dale Westby at Baue's. Your early teachings, your help waking me up and inspiring me to be better, meant the world to me over the years, and I thank you for your guidance, your brutal honesty, and most of all, your support and love during the tough times when I needed you the most.

To my more current role models, guides, and advisors, John Schmitz, CPA, and his wife, Cindy, who helped me so much with helping Baue grow and as I transitioned Baue into the Park Lawn family. To Brad Green, Jay Dodds, and now their first female CEO at Park Lawn, Jennifer Hay, who have seen to my family business and that its people are being well cared for as it continues to leave a legacy of exemplary compassionate service to families in St. Charles County, Missouri.

To the members of the Funeral Service Symposium funeral service study group, both the former and the current men who took me in as the only woman (ever—and you need to work on this, guys!) in the group; who became like brothers to me; who pushed me, teased me, supported me, and kept me from doing sooooo many stupid things as a business owner, I am so grateful to you all. You taught me so much, you held me accountable to my business and professional goals, you went scuba diving with me, you taught me to hunt pheasants, and you helped bring a young woman into adulthood to become Bad Boots Baue, and for that, I am forever grateful for your love and the lifelong friendship you and your wives have shown me since 1987.

To the members of team Baue, many of you who have remained loyal friends and professional colleagues, even though some of you have moved on or retired. You have been an inspiration to me, with your willingness to stay and support Baue after Dad died and after I bought the business. You hung in there during the difficult years and our many challenges, and you followed some of my crazy ideas, especially when we built the 22,000-square-foot multilevel, multipurpose Funeral and Memorial Center at the cemetery, now the largest combo operation serving more than 1,200 families a year. Thank you for your helpfulness in designing Baue University as something to develop leaders at all levels of the organization. It is unlike anything built in our profession in a funeral, cremation, and cemetery company, and it is a true gift to the profession. You are the best, and you taught me to be the best, and most of all, your desire to make Baue the best was the greatest gift of all.

To Dale Westby once again, who willingly stepped up and took over our cemetery management when we had no idea how to run a cemetery. You took a sense of pride in your role as our VP of cemetery service and helped our eighty-acre memorial gardens look pristine and beautiful always.

To Pat and Neva Rankin, funeral directors, former managers, and now a deacon, funeral celebrant for Baue families, as well as trainers and mentors to new Baue team members. Your friendship and loyalty over the years mean more than you know.

To Brenda Suit, Baue's CFO and now the treasurer for Funeral Women Lead, and to Pam Gehrs, our VP of sales and marketing and now a regional sales manager with Park Lawn, two women who, when they came into our finance and operations, helped bring a new level of talent and immensely improved the culture of love and care for others on the team. To Donna Denning, our last human resources director, who taught me so much about how to better develop and care for our staff and build Baue University.

To Kelly Karavasonos, LPC, our director of grief services, who helped us found the Center for Hope and Healing and helped so many Baue families with your counseling gifts and talents.

To Kristen Ernst, MA, LPC, who now owns the Center and has grown it to become one of the top counseling organizations in St. Charles County and is also the new dean of Funeral Women Lead's Women's Leadership Academy! You are an amazing teacher and leader!

To Gordon Brokaw, our only maintenance guy in my early years, who taught me how to wash cars and clean parlors the Baue way and whose musical talents brought laughter and tears to us all. To Greg Fuller, our grounds superintendent, and all the cemetery staff who work so very hard during our freezing winters and hot muggy summers. It is not an easy job, and I appreciate and am grateful to you.

To our women managers—Amy Beth Dormire, our first woman care-center manager, and Susan Short, now in charge. You ran and still do run a tight ship, doing the hard work you do ensuring that the care of the deceased is a top priority and for making the Care Center a compassionate place to work.

To Jan Smith, who came to us as funeral director and developed herself as our first woman general manager and is now vice president of operations for a major independent firm in the Midwest.

I am so very proud of you! To Terry Schertzer, who as our general manager stuck with me during some crazy and hard times and now is back to his passion in the preplanning profession. To Kacie Derby, our smart and savvy preplanning funeral and cemetery sales manager, who has more energy than any woman I know and still finds time to balance her life well with her children and husband.

To Jennifer Crist, my right hand for so many years, who not just helped us as an executive assistant but helped make my life easier as a single mom and helped our workplace culture be a better place to be. To Jim Mac and Deonna, whose loyalty continues even in retirement as a couple who have the heart of Baue in them always. To Jeff Conderman, who came to us when he was sixteen to work in maintenance, grew himself through education to become a funeral director, a supervisor, and a promoter of all things Baue. You are like a son to me, and I could not have gotten through some of my challenges without your faith in me.

To Colby Hitchcock, who started with us in the preparation center, worked his way up to become our operations manager, continued his lifelong learning, obtained his business degree, and worked hard to develop himself into the leader he is today. Colby remains, as of this writing, the director of operations for all Baue and other funeral homes in the St. Louis region for Park Lawn. You have built an incredible team of leaders and dealt with a great deal of change during the Park Lawn transition. You have held the Baue ship together and made it better, you give back with your team to the community, and you love the profession and its people passionately. You are right where you are supposed to be, and I am very proud of you! You have continued the legacy of Baue as the best funeral, cremation, and cemetery company in the region, and I am grateful.

Thank you, team Baue, for all for the support, talents, love, and compassionate service you bring to the families of St. Charles County.

To my family—my son, John, who was Baue's VP of operations, stayed during the transition to Park Lawn and the pandemic, and was a caring and compassionate caregiver to team Baue and the families we served. You have now found your most important role as a husband to your beautiful wife, Emily, and as a parent to your adorable sons, my grandsons, Jaxon, Evan, and Owen. I am so proud that as a stay-at-home dad now working part-time in another profession, you are prioritizing your most important job as a role model to your three growing boys.

To my daughter, Erin, who worked at Baue's in high school, discovered her passion in designing and overseeing events, obtained her degree in hospitality management, and is now a successful event planner in Las Vegas. You are an amazing and busy businesswoman who is willing to work nights, days, and weekends to care for your clients' needs and still has time to have an incredibly fun life with your partner, Omari. I am so very proud of you.

To my additional set of children—not by blood but by relationship—Milva Finnegan; her husband, Kevin; their children, Myla, Melina, and Timo; and Jeff Conderman, you are all such an important part of our family, and I thank you for bringing joy and love into our lives.

To my younger brother, Paul Baue, who brought so many gifts to team Baue and shared his heart with our community for so many years. You are an incredible funeral director and preplanner bro, and I am proud to be your big sis. We had a tough year in 2024 with our brother Mark's sudden death. Know that I am here for you whenever you need me, as I know you are for me.

To my Colorado stepchildren, Daniel and Taylor Crabbs, who help me with my coaching company, my podcasts, and now the new Funeral Women Lead Foundation, in addition to being incredible parents to our grandchildren, Piper and Hudson. You are both special gifts and bring your incredible talents and Millennial "Smarts" to help me every day. To Joe and Kristen Crabbs, both educators and the parents of our newest baby granddaughter, Georgia, your love and support means so much.

To Monte, my husband, my love, and my biggest supporter and cheerleader. When I said I wanted to start a coaching company during the pandemic, you said, "Okay." When I said I wanted to write my life story and help others with leadership, you helped me realize that I could tell my story, you helped me by reading my crazy stories, and you helped me realize it was okay to share them with the world. Being the great former educator and writer you are, you helped me understand how to capture readers' hearts. When I said I wanted to start a foundation to help women in the profession that would require me to travel a bit more and invest some of our savings to help it get started, you said, "Okay." You are my rock, my shoulder to lean and cry on. You believed in me when sometimes I did not believe in myself. You push me to be better, and most of all, you love me and my children and grandchildren as if they were your own blood. You are a gift that God sent me when I was ready to give up on relationships. I thank you for loving me, accepting me, and walking by my side in our life with our blended family, pups and horses, through our sometimes sad, sometimes happy, and sometimes "sappy" crazy life filled with our travels and transitions. I love you for forever and to infinity!

About the Author

LISA BAUE'S mission is to unleash greatness in women in the funeral and deathcare profession. As the former CEO and president of Baue Funeral Homes, Crematory and Cemetery, she knows what it's like to rise in a profession that wasn't built for women.

Growing up as the granddaughter and daughter of funeral directors in small-town St. Charles, Lisa spent her childhood afternoons after school in her grandparents' house above their funeral home, exploring. Despite her interest in deathcare, she was not encouraged to enter the family business or pursue a business degree, as few women worked in funeral and deathcare in the seventies and eighties.

Lisa's commitment to championing women in funeral service is deeply personal. Her father, David C. Baue, pioneered the first women-in-funeral-service program in the history of the profession in the early 1980s, providing Lisa with role models, coaching, and mentoring at a time when very few women were active in the profession. Lisa loved the funeral profession from the moment she entered it. She found deep gratification in serving those who were mourning, and she discovered a career could also be a mission.

When Lisa's father died suddenly when she was just thirty years old, she decided to purchase the family business, making her a third-generation licensed funeral director and owner. She was faced with taking over a business laden with debt in the middle of her grief and loss. Little did she know that she would emerge from that turbulent time into a leadership role that would change her life—and, decades later, the lives of women across the country through her Funeral Women Lead Foundation.

As the only actively licensed funeral woman in the local area, Lisa worked three times as hard to gain respect and acceptance. Regardless of the task, from washing cars to shoveling snow and cleaning parlors to dusting caskets, she did whatever the business needed to be successful. She worked tirelessly while also juggling her role as mother and wife.

Lisa went on to become one of the leading owners in her profession and, with her team, built one of the most well-known, respected funeral, cremation, and cemetery companies in the Midwest. Fueled by her belief in helping others in need, she has been a lifelong volunteer. She has served in a variety of leadership positions in her local community and profession, receiving numerous awards for her service and achievement.

She sold her company in 2019 and founded her business consulting company, Your Funeral Coach, two years later. Soon after, she founded the Funeral Women Lead Foundation, dedicated to helping women become future industry leaders. She firmly believes investing in women's education and leadership is critical to the future survival of the profession. Lisa's experiences inspired her book, *Wake-Up Calls*.

Learn more about Lisa and her mission to empower women at www.funeralwomenlead.org and www.lisabaue.com.

BOARD AND COMMUNITY SERVICE

- Trustee (2020–2025), board chair (2022–2023), Funeral Service Foundation

- Secretary–treasurer, Selected Independent Funeral Homes (2017–2018)

- Board member, Selected Independent Funeral Homes (2015–2018)

- Meet the Mentors speaker, National Funeral Directors Association (NFDA; 2013)

- President, Preferred Funeral Directors International (2013–2014)

- Member, Hope Lutheran Church Parish Council (2011–2014)

- Board chair, Partners for Progress in St. Charles County (2011–2012)

- St. Charles County Athena Award member

- Member, National Public Relations Press Liaison Committee, NFDA

- Certified Stephen Leader

EARLIER COMMUNITY INVOLVEMENT

- Member and board chair, Economic Development Center of St. Charles County, Missouri (2001–2008)

- Chair, American Heart Association's Heart Walk for St. Charles County (2008)

- Board member, National Foundation of Funeral Service (1994–1997)

- Member, Founding Joint Committee of the Certified Preplanning Certification program, NFDA

- Founding President of the St. Charles Crime Stoppers Program

- Council member (2000–2011), chair (2008–2009), St. Charles County Salvation Army Council

- Member, past president, Rotary Club of St. Charles, District 6060

- Member, Oak Grove City Cemetery Board

- Chair, Salvation Army Tree of Lights Campaign (2006–2007)

- Co-chair, Passage of the St. Charles County Home Rule Charter (1992)

- Member and past president, St. Charles Business and Professional Women

- Member and past president, St. Charles Jaycee Women

HONORS AND AWARDS

- International Academy of Nobel Achievement Award (1984)

- Missouri State Business and Professional Women's Organization Young Careerist (1986)

- St. Charles County Athena Award (1993)

- St. Charles County Mental Health Council and Crider Center for Mental Health Heroes Award for Mental Health (1998)

- St. Louis Women of Achievement Award (1998)

- Youth in Need Honoree (2000)

- Dove Foundation Leadership Award (2005)

- St. Charles Chamber of Commerce Lifetime Distinguished Service Civic Award (2007)

- *St. Louis Business Journal* Businesswoman of the Year Award (2010)

- St. Charles Region Winning Women Regional Economic Development Award (2011)

- Named one of the "Top 100 St. Louisans to Know" by *Small Business Monthly* (2012)

- Greater St. Charles County Chamber of Commerce Citizen of the Year Award (2014)

- Community Living Volunteer of the Year Award (2016)

About Funeral Women Lead

FUNERAL WOMEN LEAD FOUNDATION is an organization founded by Lisa Baue, her staff, and board members. Dedicated to advancing women in the funeral and deathcare profession, the organization is a catalyst for change in a field built on care, tradition, and service. It exists to support and uplift women in the profession, who are often underrepresented in leadership and ownership despite being essential to the profession's future.

Through its programs, developed in house, the foundation offers services including mentorship and coaching; leadership training and development; a resource learning library with books, podcasts, blogs, and articles; scholarships; a membership community; and in-depth research results to help advocate for women in the profession.

Funeral Women Lead creates space for women to grow, lead, and transform the culture of the funeral service and deathcare community from the inside out. In addition to its own leadership academy and wellness summit, Funeral Women Lead gathers resources, opportunities, and support from across the profession to share with passionate women who are seeking growth. Its work is grounded in the belief that when women are empowered to lead, the entire profession becomes more compassionate, inclusive, visionary, and successful.

www.ingramcontent.com/pod-product-compliance
Lightning Source LLC
Chambersburg PA
CBHW030512210326
41597CB00013B/876